WINKLES AND CHAMPAGNE

Winkles and Champagne is a book about the British Music Hall. But it is certainly not a *history* or *survey* of that peculiarly British institution.

For a start, the book is lavishly illustrated with an incredible collection of photographs, programmes, song covers, bills, posters and cartoons, mainly from the author's personal collection. Which brings us to the author himself — certainly not a dry theatrical historian. He is obviously steeped in the Music Hall and its personalities, and is able to produce hilarious anecdotes about virtually all the great names. George Robey, Harry Tate, Marie Lloyd and their contemporaries are all brought alive in these pages, and we are also treated to a tour of the theatres where they appeared and an introduction to the impressarios who engaged and managed them.

Winkles and Champagne is a classic of Music Hall history — yet a highly readable and entertaining classic.

Alan Brown

THE DARK GIRL DRESS'D IN BLUE.

SUNG BY KATE HARLEY, AND
WRITTEN & SUNG BY
HARRY CLIFTON,
AT THE
LONDON MUSIC HALLS.
LONDON
PUBLISHED BY B WILLIAMS 11 PATERNOSTER ROW.

ENT STA HALL   Pr. 2/6

Winkles and Champagne

Comedies and Tragedies of the Music Hall

M. WILLSON DISHER

With Illustrations from Photographs, Programmes, Prints, Song Covers, Song Books, Bills and Posters, mainly from the Author's Collection

CEDRIC CHIVERS
PORTWAY
BATH

THE MUSIC HALL SPIRIT IN THE EIGHTEENTH CENTURY

*From a Hogarth engraving in the
collection of Mr. Giuseppe Ceci*

WITH THANKS

to

my brother, A. R. Disher, who took me to my first music-hall some years before he went to Flanders in the summer of 1914 and was killed in action;

my parents, who overcame considerable difficulties when taking me in a bath-chair to theatres and music-halls during the long illnesses of my boyhood;

my old friends of the Empire promenade and Fleet Street who made me a music-hall critic and shared with me their memories;

the Editors of many journals and other publications, notably the *Quarterly Review, Britannia and Eve,* the *Tatler,* the *Radio Times,* the *Observer,* the *Daily Telegraph,* the *Evening News,* the *Empire News,* the *Era, Variety* (U.S.), and *Music Hall Memories,* for allowing me to melt down my articles written for them;

and to Gladys Tudor-Owen, the leading publicity manager of London music-halls, for her ready help in lending photographs where there were gaps in my own collection.

M. WILLSON DISHER.

March 16, 1938.

Programme

2 HARRY FOX, "JOLLY NOSE," HISTORIC CHAIRMAN OF THE OLD MO,
DRURY LANE

"He had a nose that might shame Cyrano, and a complexion of rich old mahogany"—H. G. Hibbert

From an "Entr'acte" caricature

3 THE ROTUNDA, VAUXHALL

From "A Month's Vacation; being an account of the manner in which a JUVENILE PARTY passed their time in Baker Street with an ENTERTAINING DESCRIPTION of the PRINCIPAL PLACES OF AMUSEMENT they visited in London." Published in London about 1825

CHAPTER ONE

Overture: Taverns in the Town

SUCH curious changes occur in this ingenious century that what were once ordinary human impulses have become stranger to us than physics or mechanics. Thus the departed world's love of singing while tippling (or tippling while singing) seems as remote as the ritual of a barbaric race. Its relics are the drinking songs which nobody sings now except when sober.

To-day "Musical Club" means chamber music in a sedate hush, so unlike what it used to mean that its members would condemn as a brawl the behaviour of their forebears.

> To our Musical Club, here's long life and prosperity.
> May it flourish with us, and so on to posterity.
> May the catch, and the glass, go about and about,
> And another succeed to the bottle that's out,

was the sentiment of every true-born Englishman, from the village pothouse-loafer to the "first gentleman in Europe"; even Dr. Samuel Johnson, lacking both music and wine, contributed to it his song of "The Jocund And Hilarious Hermit":

> Hermit hoar in solemn cell,
>   Wearing out Life's evening grey;
> Smite thy bosom sage and tell,
>   What is life, and which the way?
> Thus I spoke, and speaking sigh'd,
>   Scarce repress'd the starting tear,
> When the hoary Sage replied,
>   Come my lad and drink some beer.

as well as his glee for three voices, set to a very dainty melody:

> If the man who Turnips cries,
> Cry not when his Daddy dies;
> 'Tis proof that he would rather
> Have a turnip than a Father.

There was no numbering the Harmonic, Anacreontic, Catch and Glee Clubs of town and country, in the time of George III. What the humblest were like is evident in the *Theatrical Budget* of Charles

Mathews, where the text of his monologue describes the Nightingale Club at the Cabbage and Shears. Its Rules and Regulations, chalked up over the fireplace, ordered, "That every Gentleman must sing a Volunteer song, whether he can or no, or drink a pint of salt and water," and Mr. President saw that this was enforced.

What the most exalted was like appears in Henry Angelo's memories of a night at the Neapolitan Club, Thatched House Tavern, St. James's Street, when the Prince of Wales (afterwards George IV) and the Duke of York attended. Their brother, the Duke of Sussex, was

AN ILLUSTRATION FOR THE SONG "MY MASTER'S DRUM"
From the London Singer's Magazine

the president: he commanded, "Look to the heel-taps," and was himself "every moment putting wine into his glass" during the eight hours they were at table. The guests included Sir Sidney Smith, hero of Acre, Sheridan, "Anacreon" Moore, Beau Brummell, and a dwarf whom the Prince sat upon his knee where "like a child on the nurse's lap, he sat eating cakes and ice." The Prince sang with considerable taste and humour, and Moore sang his own "Irish Melodies," but "The Alderman's Thumb," called for by the chairman, was the ballad liked above all:

> What a noise and what a din,
> How they glitter round the Chin,
> Give me Fowl, give me Fish,
> Now for some of that nice Dish,

> Cut me this, cut me that,
>> Send me crust, and send me Fat,
>> More Fat, more Fat,
> Some for Titbits pulling, hauling,
>> Legs, Wings, Breast, Head,
> Some for Liquor scolding, bawling,
>> Hock, Port, white, red,
> Here 'tis cramming, cutting, slashing,
>> There ye Grease and Gravy splashing.
>> Look, Sir, what you've done,
> Zouns, Sir, you've cut off the Alderman's Thumb,
>> Oh! my Thumb, my Thumb,
>> Oh! my Thumb, my Thumb.

Between the Nightingale and the Neapolitan there were musical clubs for every station in life of a strictly ordered society. For tradesmen there were the Thursday nights of the Nag's Head in the Poultry, praised by Jerry Sneak in Foote's "The Mayor of Garratt" (at the Haymarket, 1763) as a haunt of "roaring, rare boys." Near Sadler's Wells the performers of that famous musick-house held theirs at the Sir Hugh Myddleton Tavern, where they entertained Angelo with Spanish and French songs, feats of strength, and tricks.

Near St. Clement Danes "choice spirits" were ruled over at the Court of Comus—admittance sixpence—by a wild young chairman named Cussans, celebrated for the exploit of riding in stage regimentals to a review of troops in Hyde Park, joining the party of King George III and the Prince of Wales as they passed along the line, and disturbing the gravity of all with his heroic aspect and stern manner.

Each night when he arrived at the Court of Comus, and was handed his cocked hat by the sergeant-at-arms to the sound of a fanfare, he sang couplets about everybody present in the manner that many an improvisatore—including Sloman, the original of young Nadab in *The Newcomes*—has copied since. Everyone in turn was called upon to "do something." Since indulgences and absolutions could only be bought at the price of half a crown, which was "considerably beyond the reach of the generality of sinners," this was imperative. George Raymond (biographer of Elliston who attended this Court) said it meant a speech, poising a tobacco-pipe or coal-scuttle, an imitation of a cat, dog, or fowl, posturizing or quaffing to the dregs a deep pewter pot of "some potent compound."

On gala nights, as the clock of St. Clement Danes struck twelve, Cussans rolled on the sanded floor, imitating a dancing-bear. A lasso was flung round him by his trainer, who beat the bottom of a pewter pot with a marrow-bone while clarionet and trumpet brayed. Cussans jigged and capered until "the poor excitement which drunkenness had produced left him at length as lifeless as an unburied corpse." Yet at

AN IRISH SONG-FRONT OF ABOUT 1800

Sadler's Wells he was a considerable actor, celebrated for singing "Oh! Poor Robinson Crusoe." One night, after singing it three or four times, he sat in the gallery to watch the rest of the perform-

4 VAUXHALL GARDENS

Interior of the Banqueting Hall

5 CREMORNE

From contemporary prints

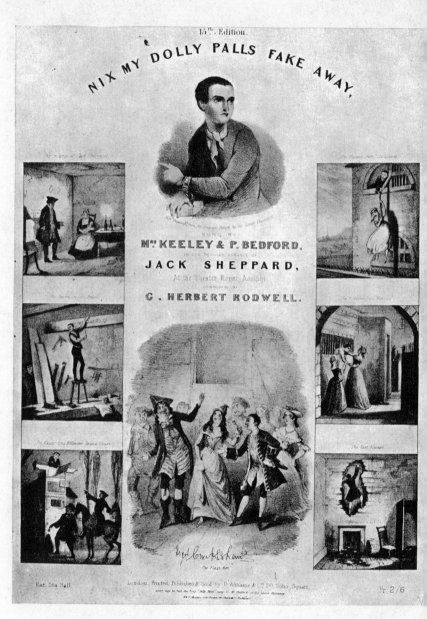

6 A SONG-FRONT WITH SCENES FROM THE PLAY OF "JACK SHEPPARD"

ance. When the curtain rose on another piece in the bill, he stood up and sang "Oh! Poor Robinson Crusoe" once more. Nor would the audience suffer the players on the stage to begin until he had sung it again on the same spot, and then again.

While the fire that burned Ned Kean was setting the enthusiasm of Drury Lane ablaze, "clubs" were talked of afresh. Kean's favourite was the Coal Hole in Fountain Court, Strand, where he formed the Wolf Club: and there he sang "Sweet Kitty Clover" to the tune composed by himself. To Cribb's in Panton Street—run by the prizefighter nicknamed "The Black Diamond" because he had been a coal-porter—Byron came late one night, to discover why Kean had stealthily left a solemn social gathering. There were such haunts of song as these all the way from Temple Bar to St. James's when Thackeray brought away from them ideas for scenes in *The Newcomes* and *Pendennis*. By then every tavern of note in the East as well as the West End had a music licence. Among the number mentioned in *The Momus and Vocal Visitor*, published in 1833, are several at addresses still well known, including the "Royal Standard (J. Moy's), Vauxhall Road," now the Victoria Palace, and the "Turkish Saloon (Cook's) Great Mogul, Drury Lane," now the Winter Garden Theatre. Savile House, now the Empire, Leicester Square, is described as "a similar establishment to the New Grecian Saloon and White Conduit House"; it must, therefore, have been considerably more than a concert-room in a tavern, and a serious rival to the Sans Souci Theatre, near by.

At most of these concerts Thomas Hood's ballads were popular. Although grimmer than others in their humour, they followed the prevailing fashion of prolonged narrative. Songs with anything from eight to twelve verses, each with a chorus of "Rooral looral" or "Doo-dle dum," make dull reading; it has to be borne in mind that they were acted, often violently acted, as well as sung, calling for efforts of arms and legs as well as vocal chords. "Nix My Dolly Palls Fake Away," the lively flash (thieves' slang) song from a stage version of Harrison Ainsworth's "Jack Sheppard" in 1839, was different: it still has an exhilarating lilt. Nearly all the ordinary comic songs of the period (right up to the time when the last of their singers vanished together midway through the 'sixties) resembled musical monologues.

In *The Show Folks*, dated 1831, Pierce Egan admits a liking for the Kean's Head, formerly the O.P. in Russell Court, Drury Lane; at its harmonic meetings on Saturday evenings Beuler was one of the singers. And there also was Tom Hudson, a grocer's apprentice before he became a sober, industrious writer of simple-hearted verses —he published a fresh little book of them each year, and sold copies to his audiences—about matrimony, conundrums, topics of the day, cockney courtships, and the state of the trade. Later he went to the

Coal Hole, and thence to the Cyder Cellars in Maiden Lane. Other singers at Sadler's Wells and the Rotunda of Vauxhall Gardens made his songs popular, but he could not earn money enough for his wife and children before he died in 1884, at the age of fifty-one. Thus those who escaped the vortex which whirled Cussans and Kean away were yet exhausted. Such was the fate also of Grimaldi, whose health was shattered before he was middle-aged. A tavern comforted his

Publish'd Sept. 5, 1808, by LAURIE & WHITTLE, 53, Fleet Street, London.

FROM THE SONG SHEET OF GRIMALDI'S "A BULL IN A CHINA SHOP"

last years. He was carried pick-a-back to a parlour, where he would recall the many comic songs he had set thousands singing at Sadler's Wells in the full glory of his clownship.

Catch and Glee Clubs,[1] including one at the Thatched House Tavern, survived until the 'forties. Later than that the Coal Hole and the Cyder Cellars became notorious for the Judge and Jury Club of Renton Nicholson, who conducted mock trials as "Lord Chief Baron." From a pawnbroker's apprentice he had expanded at tavern concerts, partly because of his coarse but ready humour and partly

---

[1] Provincial cities carried them on until the 'nineties, when "Glee Dinners," relic of all this enthusiasm for part-singing, ceased to be part of London life.

because of his "unusually developed whiskers," into a wit. He died in 1861, at the age of fifty-two; and for years afterwards tales were told about town of his admirable gravity when declaring that the court might drink and smoke. In the *Night Side of London*, published in 1858 as a warning against nocturnal joys, an enterprising moralist who left none untasted, reports that at Judge and Jury Clubs the case was invariably one of seduction or crim. con. Female witnesses were men dressed in women's clothes, and "everything was done that could be to pander to the lowest propensities of depraved humanity." The moralist did not believe the audience "could have stood this if it had not been for the drink."

By this time the amateurs of the music clubs were gone. Whereas Cussans had been paid with "a pickled herring, some strong waters, and an ounze of tobacco," the chairman of tavern concerts now wanted a weekly wage. Even singers expected money, being encouraged in this hope by the success some of them had when engaged for harmonic halls and assembly rooms. Concerts at places like these bore a

RENTON NICHOLSON
From "Painted Faces"

closer resemblance to "variety" than the serious, almost solemn, programmes of the first music-halls. To make the subject still more bewildering, the Bower Saloon in Stangate styled itself a "music-hall" while presenting a mixed bill of burlettas.

Origins form a maze we might easily get lost in before starting to trace how songs sung in taverns sprouted into "palaces of variety." Still, you should know that such growth was the natural order of things. Round about 1700, tipplers in the tavern of Sadler's Wells were entertained by the waiter and other odd performers, so that it grew into a "musick-house," admittance by ticket which entitled the holder to its face value in liquor. When the Wells changed into a theatre, others supplied the old demand for song and dance. It was

JUDGE & JURY
SOCIETY,
COAL HOLE TAVERN,
FOUNTAIN COURT, STRAND,
OPPOSITE EXETER HALL.

THE LORD CHIEF BARON
NICHOLSON

Has the honour to remind his best Friends, the Public, that he presides over his

MIMIC COURT OF LAW
EVERY NIGHT.

Proceedings commence at Half-past Nine o'clock.

POSES PLASTIQUES
EVERY EVENING, AT HALF-PAST SEVEN, AND AFTER THE THEATRES.

CHOPS, STEAKS, &c. Dressed in the COFFEE ROOM.

AN ORDINARY DAILY, AT SIX O'CLOCK.

Private Rooms for Dinner and Supper Parties.

BEDS, 1s. 6d.

The jolly old Baron will merrily quaff,
Presiding as geni o'er learning and chaff,
In the court where old Momus o'er sorrow prevails,
Yet Justice holds fairly her sword and her scales.

Printed by J. W. PEEL's Steam Machine, 74, New Cut, Lambeth.

Aug.ᵗ 1855.

A CONTEMPORARY HAND-BILL

8

then that the Grecian Saloon grew out of the Eagle Tavern in the City Road, and the Britannia Saloon out of the Britannia Tavern in Hoxton (with "Variety Entertainment" on its bills in 1841). When these in turn became theatres (the Act of 1843 enabling them to do so), where was the London public to satisfy its old desires? That was how the widespread music-hall boom began, bringing into existence a new community, united by a destiny of sudden wealth, who were worshipped as idols, and given the name of "stars."

When we talk of the music-hall, disregarding earlier existence of the name and the thing, we mean not bricks-and-mortar or variety entertainment of any time and place, but these free souls—so many of whom demonstrated how

> Golden lads and girls all must,
> As chimney-sweepers, come to dust.

Short as life was for them, it was too long for their powers of reckoning.

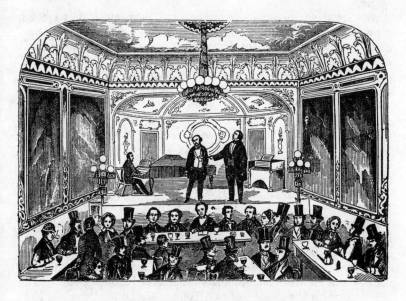

THE LORD RAGLAN MUSIC HALL

From "Paul Pry," Jan. 17, 1857

CHAPTER TWO

"Beginners, Please"

"GIVE your orders, gentlemen, please!" The chairman cannot make himself heard. "*Orders, gents.*" His tone insists that as the cost of the entertainment comes out of the sale of food and drink, there can be no more songs if there is no more supper. "ORDERS, GENTS." This is clearly a threat that unless tankards are more hastily emptied and refilled, he will stay the glees and catches. Somebody at his own table calms him by asking (yet again) what he will have: he answers, raps on the table with his hammer, and announces the next singer.

Most of the audience are tradesmen and mechanics; they smoke pipes, drink porter and like to keep their money for their wives. But these Saturday nights at the Canterbury Arms, by the railway arch in Westminster Bridge Road, are so popular that the public-house is crowded out. Charles Morton, the landlord, starts Thursday nights as well, and they too are crowded out. In less than a year he builds a hall over his skittle alley big enough for seven hundred people, admittance by ticket that pays for refreshment. It is opened in 1849, and thrives so well it has to be grandly rebuilt. Henceforth the term "music-hall" means the "music-hall of a tavern." At the Canterbury music is taken very seriously—Gounod's *Faust* is sung for the first time in London, and Mme Tietjens comes to hear it. Also, a picture gallery is added—known as "The Academy-Over-the-Water."

Every publican would now try to lay violent hands on the building next door, whether workshop or stable-yard, school or church. No opera house was too grand for the purpose and no shanty too mean. Weston's (now the Holborn Empire) was constructed out of the Holborn National School Rooms. The South London usurped the site of a Roman Catholic chapel. The Oxford arose, in Oxford Street, in the yard of the Boar and Castle. The London Pavilion had been another stable-yard until an exhibition of anatomical waxworks put a roof over it, and was next a skating-rink before the music-hall chairman claimed it. Later, the Trocadero, named after a palace in the Paris Exhibition which had been named after a fort at Cadiz, took the place of the

8 THE ADVENT OF THE AGE OF SPEED

(On Reverse) 7 THE DANCING PLATFORM AT CREMORNE

notorious [1] Argyll Rooms at the top of the Haymarket. Even the Pantheon in Oxford Street, beneath whose eighteenth-century portico fifty gallants with drawn swords had escorted Mrs. Baddeley from her Sedan chair and forced the manager down upon his knees to crave pardon for barring actresses from the masquerades, was pressed into service.

As the halls multiplied, so the need for singers increased. Mechanics, dishwashers, scrubbers, lawyers' clerks, and actors took part in this gold rush. Amateurs who had been content to sing for the sake of taproom applause became aware that the ability to amuse might be worth a weekly wage up to a hundred pounds. They packed their carpet-bags and trudged miles wherever trial turns were given a hearing. There they would wait, lined up in wind and rain, because there was no room for them all behind the scenes.

Each on being beckoned would raddle his face in a small room

CHARLES MORTON
From "Stage Whispers," a "Judy" Shilling book

occupied by a dozen other seekers after fame. With little warning, he would suddenly find himself pushed on to a little platform in front of a surging crowd roused to blood lust. If not stunned by a bottle while striving to recover from stage-fright, he might get to the end

---

[1] Not to be confused with the Argyll Rooms of Regent Street, where musical history had been made amid masquerades and acrobatics. These were near the site of the Palais Royal, a casino, where Hengler's Cirque was built in 1871 (rebuilt in 1885) and the Palladium in the December of 1910.

of the first verse. Cat-calls, boos, old boots, and a dead cat might come his way. Perhaps, though this was unlikely, he might be encouraged. By far the wisest thing he could do would be to break into a clog-dance, partly to soothe the savage breasts and partly to make himself a moving target. In industrial areas iron rivets were usually flung. In London galleries the bottles carried round by waiters were chained to the trays. In many halls, steel grills had to be stretched over the unoffending orchestra.

THE LORD NELSON TAVERN
From "Paul Pry," Nov. 29, 1856

Hundreds retired heart-broken, if not maimed, from the struggle. Dozens received bottles and vegetables as presents instead of missiles, and trod the Milky Way. One day a drudge, the next a star. That was the experience of many. They rose so suddenly to wealth and worship that they had no time to accustom themselves to their new life. They were children on holiday, eager to spend all their pocket-money before the fun should cease. In the midst of the Victorian world whose first law was that every man, woman, child, and beast should know his or her place, they had the licence of court jesters to go where they pleased. As *lions comiques, buffo vocalists,* and *serio comics,* they blazed into stars at a time when the singers of the song-and-supper rooms were vanishing. Sam Collins was one of the older band. You may have stopped by his grave at Kensal Green to look at his Irish hat and shillelagh carved on the tombstone, and you may have been to the music-hall at Islington Green which still bears his

THE OXFORD,

6, OXFORD STREET, NEAR TOTTENHAM COURT ROAD.

OPEN EVERY EVENING.

Admission: Hall, 6d.   Balcony & Stalls, 1s.   Private Boxes, 10s. 6d.

9   A HAND-BILL OF 1861

name. He was a chimney-sweep before appearing at Evans's Song-and-Supper Rooms in Covent Garden (remembered by this generation as the National Sporting Club), to sing "Paddy's Wedding" and "Limerick Races." He died at the age of thirty-nine in the spring of 1865.

Singers who thrived at Evans's on "a guinea a week and supper each night," ran to the devil on thirty or forty pounds a week at music-halls. Sam Cowell, who came from the Grecian and Cremorne (where revellers in the dining-room poured champagne from the balconies upon crowds below), was one. From Evans's, where he sang "Villikins And His Dinah," "The Rat-Catcher's Daughter," "Billy Barlow " (so popular that the name was adopted by an English actress, an Australian comedian, and an American minstrel), and burlesques of "Alonzo," "Blue Beard," and "Macbeth," he went to the newly opened Canterbury and was offered engagements at the Oxford before it was built. Thus he would have been the father of music-hall comedians had he not toured America, where the spirits he drank when times were bad, and the illness he contracted while starving on long journeys when times were worse still, ruined his health before his return. His end was told in this account from Blandford, near Pool, in Dorset :

Sam Cowell had constant engagements and was well paid. What more? Only the common story—"unbounded applause," unwholesome living, drink, broken health. Said our host of the Crown one day (being up in London and knowing all these celebrities) "You're not looking well, Sam ; come down to Blandford and we'll set you right again." Some months after which, a ghostly, pale man arrived at the Crown in the railway omnibus, and this was the celebrated Mr. Cowell. The waiter and chambermaids regarded him with curiosity : the stablemen talked of him over their beer : his arrival made more or less sensation throughout the town. He was very ill, grew worse and worse ; consumed a bottle of brandy per diem, when he could get it, and was somewhat noisy. At length, the Crown's hospitality being worn out, though not the host's kindness, a lodging was taken in the town and the sick man's wife brought from London. He was carried downstairs in an arm-chair : and next and lastly, before many days, his body was laid in the cemetery, among those Dorset fields and orchards. A little subscription was made for his wife and children, and a stone placed over his grave. Some well-meaning people had administered ghostly consolation of the usual kind to the poor Grotesque, and his last words were : "Safe ! safe !" On his tomb is engraved : "Here lies all that is mortal of Sam Cowell. Born April 5th, 1819. Died March 11th, 1864."

In the following August, Frederick Robson, the original singer of "Villikins," died at the age of forty-three. He sang it first at the Grecian, then in Dublin, where he taught it to Toole, and lastly, in

The Wandering Minstrel at the Olympic, where he was hailed by all as "the greatest genius since Edmund Kean," before drink was the

A VICTORIAN PROGRAMME COVER

end of him too. Success killed him, because he feared it would not last. He was a genius who considered himself a fraud. Then there was W. G. Ross, a Glasgow compositor, who became famous at the Cyder Cellars. Among his earlier songs were "The Lively Flea"

and "Pat's Leather Breeches"; but these were nothing to the stir
he created with

> My name it is Sam Hall, Chimney Sweep.
> My name it is Sam Hall.
> I robs both great and small,
> But they make me pay for all,
>   D—n their eyes.

It was the outburst of a condemned criminal so full of "brutal ferocity
and pent-up fury" as to make some of his audience shudder. Yet he
dwindled one Christmas in the 'seventies into a pantomime Father
Christmas at Sanger's Amphitheatre across Westminster Bridge, and
then into a super at the Philharmonic, Islington, before ending his
days as a chorus singer in Gaiety burlesques.

One of that group lived happily ever afterwards. E. W. Mackney,
the celebrated Negro Delineator, who sang at Evans's on the same
nights as Cowell, died in 1909, aged eighty-four. Thoughts of him
take us back to the first music-halls when the proprietor was the
chairman. One night at Weston's a misguided enthusiast threw
Mackney half a crown. Weston stood up, made a long speech of
protest, pointed out what an unwarrantable liberty had been taken,
fervently hoped that such an abominable thing would never happen
again, and called for the head waiter. "Pick up that half-crown, sir,"
he said, "and throw it, sir, in the till."

What the audiences in the 'sixties looked like depended on the eye
of the beholder. The *Observer* described them as mixed crowds of
folly and vice, where youth was ensnared by the heartless skittle sharp
and blackleg, the patrician *roué*, and the plebeian "fancy man." And
Punch asked whether the music-hall was the place for a gentleman to
go to, or even for a greengrocer, a chimney-sweep, or costermonger,
or any man who entertained a liking to be thought respectable, and
recommended Evans's, where there was music in the singing, instead.
The scandal was less severely described by Emily Soldene in a lively
picture of the Oxford, which she considered a magnificent structure
in the Italian style, with frescoes, gilding, and lots of light:

Bars down the side were dressed with plenty of flowers, coloured glass, and
any amount of bright, glittering, brass-bound barrels and bottles. But, after
all, the brightest, most glittering, and most attractive thing about the bars (of
course, not counting the drinks) were the barmaids. Rows of little tables, at
which people sat and smoked, and drank, filled the auditorium, and in and out
the tables circulated the peripatetic, faded, suggesting, inquiring, deferential
waiter, and the brisk, alert, "cigar," "programme," and "book of words " boy.

Gay society consisted of "Chappies" and "Johnnies," racing men
and "Daughters of Joy." Lest people should think excess of fortune

THE CANTERBURY IN ITS EARLY DAYS

From a contemporary song-sheet

16

12 "UP AND DOWN THE CITY ROAD, IN AND OUT THE EAGLE"

From a contemporary print

13 W. G. ROSS AS SAM HALL

Then I hit 'im on the 'ead
With a d—n great lump of lead
And I left 'im there for dead.
    D—n his eyes.
            From a lithograph sold at the Cyder Cellars

and drink had hardened the hearts of these poor girls, Emily Soldene tells how "many a night have I, 'by request,' sung 'Home, Sweet Home,' because 'I made 'em cry.'" The "profitable clique" round the chairman's table were the hardest to please, and with it went the hammer of the chairman, "a most stimulating and directing factor in giving 'a lead' to public opinion and applause." So the Oxford remained until one February night in 1868: Charles Morton, while passing that way by chance, saw in a window the beginnings of a blaze that burned the building down. The second Oxford was burned down and the last pulled down.

One other joy of the old music-halls must be recalled. When Emily Soldene described how Charles Morton would himself "break the succulent potato on to the customer's plate, where it fell in a snowy shower, sweet-smelling, soft, floury and hot, ye gods, so hot!" she shows an interest in baked potatoes typical of those times and lost awhile.

EVANS'S SONG-AND-SUPPER ROOMS IN 1860
From Sala's "Twice round the Clock"

CHAPTER THREE

Enter the Lion Comique

THERE never has been another community like the old idols of the halls who drank champagne with princes in palaces, ate winkles with their old friends round street stalls, and among themselves swallowed champagne, whelks and winkles together. If kind hearts and simple faith are as precious as the poet declared them to be, these were the salt of mid-Victorian society. The *serio comic*, in her hours of ease, would not only smooth pillows, but scrub the floors for her sick friends, and the *lion comique* would fetch a sack of coal and another of potatoes in his own carriage-and-pair to an old penniless neighbour. That still happened in their hey-day in the 'nineties when Albert Edward, Prince of Wales, was glad to meet them, hear them sing, and give them jewelled tie-pins.

Among the *lions comiques* was the Great Vance, originally Alfred Peck Stevens, who walked out of a solicitor's office in Lincoln's Inn Fields and into a stage-door. When singing became more profitable than acting, he went on the boards with :

> I'm a chickaleery bloke with my one, two, three,
> Vitechapel was the willage I was born in ;
> To catch me on the hop, or upon my tibby drop,
> You must get up werry early in the morning.

That followed the Cockney style of Sam Cowell without any attempt to be leonine. The heavy swell who went on the spree was not invented until a mechanic from the Midlands came to London for work, sang in the East End as Joe Saunders, and was set by Charles Morton before the worshipping eyes of the Canterbury as George Leybourne or Champagne Charlie. On the stage he was as gilded as Lord Dundreary. Off the stage he was carried away by the industrial holiday fever of the wakes. "The whole duty of man is to earn all he can in order to spend all he can," would express his outlook on life. His year's engagement at the Canterbury at twenty-five pounds a week gave him a taste for champagne, a glistening topper, and a great-coat with the largest fur collar in London. He rode with pretty creatures in his own carriage-and-pair—a carriage-and-four in times

18

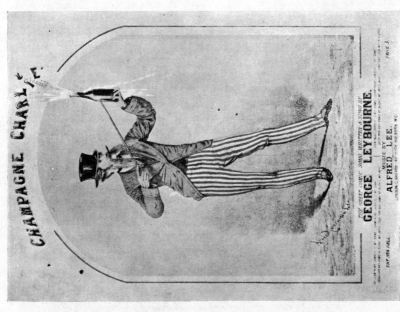

14, 15 THE RIVAL LIONS

17 VANCE: "DOING THE ACADEMY IS
QUITE THE THING YOU KNOW"

From uncoloured song-fronts

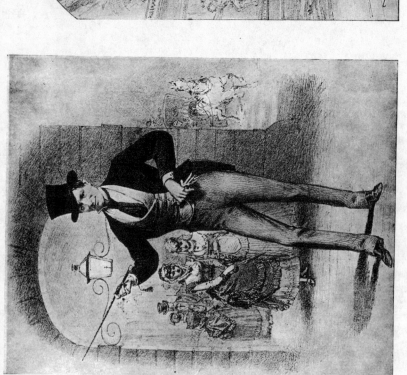

16 LEYBOURNE: "NIGHT IS THE TIME
TO HAVE A SPREE, MY BOYS"

of advertisement. One of his rivals, to ridicule him, drove a cart and four donkeys.

In "Champagne Charlie" he voiced sentiments so agreeable to rebels against Victorian respectability that his salary went up to £120 a week. Before his audience in the evenings he wore fantastic clothes of many colours, decorated his face with monocle and whiskers, and exhorted his hearers to be with the boys "who make a noise from now till day is dawning." At night he took his own advice. Every day was a holiday; his pockets filled as soon as they emptied.

The success of Vance, who imitated him with "Cliquot, Cliquot, That's The Wine For Me," increased his own. Together they went through the list with "Moët And Chandon's The Wine For Me," "Cool Burgundy Ben," "Sparkling Moselle," and "Our Glorious English Beer." Then Vance began a craze for righteous fervour with "Act On The Square, Boys, Act On The Square," one of many "motto songs." These were specially favoured by Harry Clifton, although he would unbend in "The Weepin' Willer Or The Miller's Daughter," words and music by himself:

> Then she did prepare,
> Her mortal life to injure,
> Her head was bare and the colour of her hair
> Was a sort of delicate ginger————Auburn.

Harry Clifton had a holy fervour when singing about helping a weary brother in "Pulling Hard Against The Stream," or loving your neighbour as yourself in "Paddle Your Own Canoe." Although there was a large number of comic songs in his repertoire, it was dominated by the exhortatory style of "Work, Boys, Work, And Be Contented" and (still more unwearying in moral zeal) "Try To Be Happy And Gay, My Boys." This mood affected all the idols of the halls. They were strictly moral in principle, however reckless they might be in practice. Judged by virtues that are the heart's test, they were as good as bread.

Like the rest, Leybourne spent money as freely on the poor as on the champagne he drank out of pewter pots to wash down plates of whelks. That he had an instinct for kindly acts his treatment of Jenny Hill shows. She was the daughter of a cabbie on a Marylebone rank, who thought it would be a fine thing for his girl if she learnt the trade of a *serio comic,* and apprenticed her to a North Country publican. In return for the privilege of singing to farmers until two in the morning, she had to get up at 5 a.m. in order to scrub floors, polish pewter, and bottle beer until the performance began again at noon. She married an acrobat (who taught her his trade so vigorously that she felt the effects to the end of her life), and when barely out

of her 'teens she was stranded with a baby. She waited day after day
in the agents' offices, until one sent her with a note to the Pavilion.
The manager read, "Don't trouble to see the bearer. I have merely
sent her up to get rid of her. She's troublesome," and decided to
give her a chance. That night she "stopped the show." Leybourne,
waiting in the wings, took her in his arms and held her up to the full
view of the tables.

As "The Vital Spark," Jenny Hill earned enough by dancing the
"Cellar Flap," by her song as "The Coffee-Shop Girl," and by her
"male impersonations," to buy The Hermitage and its farmlands at
Streatham. When Tony Pastor, the leading music-hall manager of
America, came over to arrange her visit to New York, she gave a
party, described by H. G. Hibbert in *Fifty Years of a Londoner's Life*,
in his honour :

> To The Hermitage that summer Sunday went every music-hall celebrity
> of the day. The arrivals began at ten o'clock in the morning, and everyone
> was greeted under the Stars and Stripes with a freshly opened pint of cham-
> pagne. There was a luncheon ; there was afternoon tea in the grounds, there
> was a dinner, with many speeches, and there were early morning travellers to
> London by the workmen's trains. But, indeed, there was no note so human
> as Bessie Bellwood's shriek of delight when she heard a hawker crying winkles
> down the lane. His stock, on a japanned tea-tray slung round his neck, was
> promptly commandeered. The shocked footman, handing round tea, was
> despatched for pins ; and the immortal singer of "Wot Cheer, Riah," whose
> real name was Mahoney, and who claimed to be a descendant of "Father
> Prout" but who, most certainly, began life as a rabbit-skinner in the New
> Cut, carefully divided her spoils among many applicants.

Little is remembered of Bessie Bellwood because her fame has been
overshadowed. But she was the rowdiest dare-devil of the lot.
Within four hours of a conversation with Cardinal Manning about
some Catholic charity, she was arrested for knocking a cabman
down in Tottenham Court Road because he had insulted (or rather
because she fancied he had insulted) her man. She sang a song :

> What cheer, Riah !
>   Riah's on the job,
> What cheer Riah !
>   Did she speculate a bob ?
> Now Riah she's a toff
> And she looks immensikoff,
> So it's what cheer Riah, Riah,
>   Hi ! Hi ! Hi !

which was wafted into every quarter of the town, including royal
palaces, so Arthur Roberts says in *Fifty Years of Spoof*. Word was

brought to him that Princess Louise and other members of the Court were "just dying" to hear her sing it. A charity matinée was organised for the purpose, at the house of an enthusiast whose husband objected so strongly that he had himself locked in his library. When Bessie arrived bedraggled, the butler gazed at her in horror until she examined him with care, and said sorrowfully, "Gor' blimey! Where 'ave they found it." To "see if he was real" she pinched his legs and stuck a pin through his wig, until he screamed like a frightened child, and lost the key of the library.

"Surely a veritable Jekyll and Hyde among comediennes," was how Arthur Roberts described her. Among the poor she was known for her kindness of heart in giving them (literally) all her worldly goods, nursing the sick, washing and scrubbing for them, and paying to have masses sung for the souls of the dead.

What happened when she made her first appearance at the

JENNY HILL
From "Painted Faces"

Star, Bermondsey, was described a few years after it had happened by Jerome K. Jerome in *The Idler Magazine* for March 1892. She had been engaged as a deputy for some local favourite, and was announced by the chairman as Signorina Ballatino, the world-famous performer on the zithern. To a large coalheaver who at once protested, he said, "You, sir, in the flannel shirt. I can see you. Will you allow this' lady to give her entertainment?"

"No," was the answer.

"Then, sir," said the chairman, "you are no gentleman." The

signorina took charge. Telling the chairman to shut up if that was all he could do, she came down to the footlights.

Thereupon ensued a slanging match the memory of which sends a thrill of admiration through me even to this day. It was a battle worthy of the gods. He was a heaver of coals, quick and ready beyond his kind. But as well might the lamb stand up against the eagle when the shadow of its wings falls across the green pastures, and the wind flies before the dark oncoming. At the end of two minutes he lay gasping, dazed and speechless.

After announcing her intention of "wiping down the bloomin' 'all" with him, and making it "respectable," she began, and the people sitting near him drew away, leaving him alone, "surrounded by space and language." She spoke for five and three-quarter minutes by the clock without a pause :

At the end, she gathered herself together for one supreme effort, and hurled at him an insult so bitter with scorn, so sharp with insight into his career and character, so heavy with prophetic curse, that strong men drew and held their breath while it passed over them, and women hid their faces and shivered. Then she folded her arms and stood silent, and the house, from floor to ceiling, rose and cheered her until there was no more breath left in its lungs.

Through the good services of an agent, she was given a trial at the Holborn. In a chastened mood, posing as "the guileless daughter of Erin," she sang, "Come Under My Umbrella." The manager, turning fiercely on the agent, said, "She won't do. She's too quiet." Some years afterwards she ran across the stage of the Tivoli without her skirt and petticoats—for a wager—telling "the boys" to take no notice of her "round the houses."

Jolly John Nash, remembered as the singer of "Sister Mary Walks Like This," was equally unabashed. When appearing at a private party before the Prince of Wales (Edward VII), he was told by the duke in whose house they were, to take off his hat and keep it off. He began his reply with the words, "Mr. Chairman," which the whole company repeated at intervals throughout the evening. He asked whether he might sing his song as though in a music-hall, and was told to keep his hat on by the guests. On coming to the chorus, he cried, "Now then, Mr. Chairman, chorus—all together," and they all sang with more spirit, though considerably less ear, than the Neapolitan Club at the Thatched House Tavern :

> Hi ! Hi ! Here stop !
> Waiter, Waiter, Fizz pop !
>   I'm rackety Jack,
>   No money I lack,
> And I'm the boy for a spree.

18 W. B. FAIR

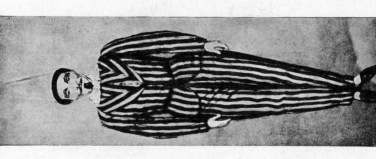

19 JAMES HENRY STEAD

20 JOLLY JOHN NASH

From coloured song-fronts

MISS BESSIE BELLWOOD.

THE BARMAID WHO SAYS SHE ONLY GIVES PEOPLE WHAT THEY WANT. SHE HAS BEEN KNOWN TO GIVE A MIDDLESEX MAGISTRATE A LITTLE MORE THAN HE WANTS.

22   THE DARE DEVIL

21   ANNIE ADAMS

All too soon the rollicking rams departed from life, and the age of teashops began. Sir Oswald Stoll, when a boy, went to fetch Leybourne from his lodgings, with the plea, "Your friends in front are waiting for you." The *lion comique* replied, "My friends? I have no friends." At the music-hall he collapsed, but directly he dragged himself to the footlights all his old swagger returned as he sang of teashop romance in "Ting! Ting! That's How The Bell Goes!" Champagne and whelks helped him to keep his last engagements. A few days after he had struggled through a performance at the Queen's, Poplar, in 1884, he died: he was forty-four. Vance fell dead during his turn at the Sun, Knightsbridge, on the Boxing Day of 1888: he was forty-nine. Harry Clifton died in 1872, aged forty. Nelly Power, a *serio comic* who sang "The Boy I Love Sits Up In The Gallery" in a way

✦ **PROGRAMME.** ✦

For Week ending October 29th, 1892.

1	Overture.
2	Will Gilbert. *Negro Comedian.*
3	Edwin Boyde. *Comedian.*
4	Florrie Robina. *Serio-Comic and Dancer.*
5	Austin Rudd. *Comedian.*
6	Ida Heath. *Transformation Dancer.*
7	Fred Mason. *Comedian.*
8	Tennyson & O'Gorman *Irish Comedians.*
9	George Beauchamp. *Comedian.*
10	Eugene Stratton. *Negro Comedian.*
11	Florence Levey. *Serio-Comic and Dancer.*
12	Harry Pleon. *Comedian.*
13	Leo Stormont. *Baritone Vocalist.*
14	Kate James. *Comedienne.*
15	The Tiny Websters. *Lilliputian Wonders.* Aged 22 & 20.
16	Herbert Campbell *Comedian.*
17	Albert Chevalier. *Comedian.*
18	Minnie Cunningham. *Serio-Comic and Dancer.*
19	Severus Schäffer. *Juggler and Equilibrist.*
20	Sam Redfern. *Comedian.*
21	Josephine Henley. *Serio-Comic.*
22	Marie Leyton. *American Serpentine Dancer.*
23	Harry Randall. *Comedian.*
24	Bessie Bellwood. *Comedienne.*
25	R. G. Knowles. *Comedian.*
26	Arthur Forrest. *Comedian.*
27	Tom Bass. *Comedian.*
28	Johnny Dwyer. *Comedian.*

The above Programme is subject to alteration.

MATINEE EVERY SATURDAY AT 2.30.

Acting Manager	... ...	MR. CHARLES MORTON.
Stage Manager	... ...	MR. VERNON DOWSETT.
Musical Director	... ...	MR. ANGELO A. ASHER.

A TIVOLI PROGRAMME

that made every boy in the gallery wish it were he, died in 1887, at the age of thirty-two. That Vital Spark, Jenny Hill, became an invalid whose chief interest in life was her albums of press-cuttings: she died in 1896 at the age of forty-six. Bessie Bellwood died the same year, at the age of thirty-nine. Thus the genius of a second generation of singers burned itself out.

Even the Great Macdermott, who suffered no harrowing days, was but fifty-six when he died in 1901. As G. H. Farrell he began life as a bricklayer, and was next a seaman; as Gilbert Hastings he turned actor, author, and stage-manager at the Grecian, at the Britannia, and at the Islington Grand, and as G. H. Macdermott he became a singer of peculiar celebrity until he turned himself into a music-hall manager and an agent. He is so well remembered for what has come to be called "the Jingo Song," we forget he was a comedian who joked like any other about mothers-in-law, lodgers, twins, the Salvation Army, curates, the sea-serpent, tight-lacing and shapely ankles. Like any other, he also joked about politics; unlike the others, he became the

JENNY HILL (VITAL SPARK)
From an "Entr'acte Almanack"

statesman of the halls. Rumour said that he was subsidised by the Conservatives, which might explain why he would disconcertingly praise Gladstone after a series of attacks, including "True Blues, Stand To Your Guns," with its refrain of "W.E.G.'s in a state of lunacy." In a more inspired mood he sang of Gordon's death in a ballad not without dignity, and not without a blow at Gladstone for the ending. That, too, has been forgotten. The one which is still linked with

23 A SONG-FRONT OF 1880

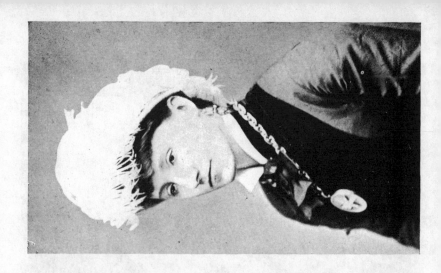

his name was written for him in 1877, soon after the outbreak of the
Russo-Turkish War, and had so strong an influence over the public
that historians have noted it. In his *Disraeli*, D. L. Murray describes
how the Tory Government triumphantly carried their vote of credit
for six millions through Parliament to oppose Russia in the Near East,
while "in the Pavilion Music Hall the glasses leapt and rattled, and in
all the streets the errand-boys went whistling truculently to the lilt
of a new song." It began:

> The Dogs of War are loose and the rugged Russian Bear,
> Full bent on blood and robbery has crawled out of his lair,

declared:

> As peacemaker Old England her very utmost tried,
> The Russians said they wanted peace, but then those Russians lied,
> Of carnage and of trickery they'll have sufficient feast,
> Ere they dare to think of coming near our Road unto the East,

and accused the Cossacks of atrocities in verses that fired patriots to
sing the chorus:

> We don't want to fight, but by jingo if we do,
> We've got the ships, we've got the men, and got the money too,
> We've fought the Bear before, and while we're Britons true,
> The Russians shall not have Constantinople.

At the time of Turkish successes Hunt prepared a new version in the
autumn of 1877, with the last line of the chorus changed to "The
Turks have proved so true, the Russians can't get near to Constantinople." But when the tide of battle turned, the singer revived the
first version before bringing out a sequel, answering those who "sneer
about Jingoes" with "If it's Jingo to love honour, then Jingoes sure
are we," to the refrain of:

> So we're waiting for the signal; directly up it runs,
> Clear the decks for action, stand by the guns,
> Our Army and our Navy, true British dogs of war,
> Will make them cry "Peccavi," the same as they did before.

The words and music were by G. H. Hunt, one of those music-hall
bards whose names remained unknown while they wrote songs, for
a guinea or two, that were to become known the world over. Highly
pleased with his war song the moment it was finished in the dead of
night, he at once knocked up Macdermott, who flung a boot at him.
This is told in *The Story of the Music Hall*, by Archibald Haddon, who
heard from Charles Coburn what the performance was like. Starting
up-stage, Macdermott would come down to the footlights "in a

E

series of dramatic little hops," each hop emphasising bulldog determination which culminated in a threatening gesture at "*Shall not have Constantinople.*" There were riots. Mobs sang "By Jingo If We Do" in the streets, at peace meetings, and outside Gladstone's house before smashing the windows. The composer, who was called "Jingo" Hunt until after his death over a quarter of a century later, has been credited with having coined that exclamation. It had been in use for centuries, and not he, but political opponents, gave "Jingo" and "Jingoism" their present meanings.

Other singers of his day are remembered by a single song. One of them is W. B. Fair, because of "Tommy, Make Room For Your Uncle"—sung everywhere persistently, as Browning recorded in the lines:

> Treading down rose and ranunculus,
> You "Tommy, make room for your uncle," us,
> Troop, all of you—man or homunculus.

With a fortune made out of this song, which he sang for ten years, sometimes "working" six halls a night, Fair bought the Winchester [1] in Southwark Bridge Road, lost his money, returned to the halls as a chairman, and ended as a link-man outside the Coliseum before his death in 1909, at the age of fifty-eight.

James Henry Stead was famous for "The Cure," or rather for the way he bounced up and down rigidly to the dance music after the chorus; and Annie Adams, noisiest, largest, and most commanding of *serio comics*, for:

> He played on the Indian drum-drum-drum,
> All down the street he would come-come-come,
> He played on the Indian drum-drum-drum,
> And made a terrible noise.

Splendid dresses for her fine figure were costly. Her husband was always waiting in "first entrance" with his mouth full of pins, so that directly she came off he could preserve the hem of her velvet garment by pinning it up to keep it out of the dust.

These were a few of the stars of the 'seventies and 'eighties. How many others there were can be guessed when you know that in London alone five hundred audiences were clamouring for their songs nightly. There was to be no slackening of the demand for twenty years to come, even though the music-hall was already being

---

[1] This (opened in 1846 as the Grand Harmonic Hall) became the Surrey Music Hall before it was called the Winchester, to distinguish it from the Surrey Theatre (later the Surrey Vaudeville Theatre) near by, and the Surrey Music Hall where concerts were given in the Surrey Gardens.

supplanted. Strictly speaking, that name belongs to the tavern concert with an audience at tables—except in the gallery, where you

COVER OF A SONG BY THOMAS HUDSON

had to nurse your liquor—and a chairman in command. These conditions created that galaxy of stars who continued long after their old haunts changed in the 'nineties. There were still chairmen, and tickets were still exchanged for liquor or cigars at Collins's, Gatti's-Under-The-Arches [1] (Hungerford Bridge), Gatti's-In-The-Road (Westminster Bridge), and at halls that held two or three hundred people. But elsewhere the music-hall of the tavern was losing its peculiar atmosphere, and becoming merged into the business of mixed entertainment that had had much the same characteristics from the court of the Pharaohs to the fairs of Old England. When prosperity led to further rebuilding, what arose under the old familiar names were theatres of variety.

The Canterbury led the way in 1876, when it was transformed into a palace so splendid that the Prince of Wales came to see the ballets. Ten years later the London Pavilion became palatial (by the standards, soon to be surpassed, of its day). Next, in 1890, the Tivoli took the place of the Tivoli Lager Beer Restaurant (named after the Tivoli Gardens of Paris) in the Strand. Such improvements were typical of the early 'nineties. Sadler's Wells changed its licence from theatre to hall, and caused the doors of little Deacon's, on the opposite bank of the New River, to close ; and soon after the English Opera House in Cambridge Circus had changed into the Palace Theatre of Varieties, with Charles Morton in charge, the Trocadero's life as a music-hall ended (until, as a restaurant, it should be equipped with a stage for cabarets, which—sung before audiences at tables—caused the old spirit of wine and song to revive). Still greater changes occurred in the provinces. From the Parthenon, Liverpool, under his mother's management, a young Australian, who had adopted his stepfather's name of Stoll, set out on a campaign to change music-halls into theatres of variety. Instead of those feasts which began at 6.30 p.m. and ended at midnight, he adopted the "twice nightly" system— devised by Maurice de Frece at the Alhambra, Liverpool—of turning the audience out at round about nine o'clock and letting in a fresh one. With this idea went his ambition to dignify the character of the entertainment, to advertise which he took the name of a famous house in Leicester Square. Leveno's at Cardiff thus became the Cardiff Empire, then Swansea had an Empire, and then Stoll began to build others in England. Meanwhile, a showman named Moss, who had begun among booths and circuses at the fairs, founded an Empire at Edinburgh and came South, leaving an Empire behind him whenever he moved. When the empire-builders joined forces for the advance on London, they became Moss Empires Ltd. They founded Empires in the suburbs, but as the original Empire in Leicester Square was not for sale, the houses they built in the West End were the

---

[1] While the hall itself has become a picture theatre, one of the bars has been found large enough to be transformed into a private playhouse—the Gate Theatre Studio.

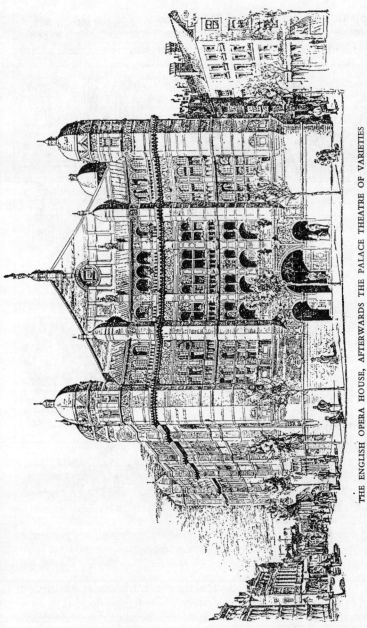

THE ENGLISH OPERA HOUSE, AFTERWARDS THE PALACE THEATRE OF VARIETIES

From "The Theatre," Feb. 1, 1891

Hippodrome, a memorial of Moss's early love of the circus, and the Coliseum, named after the Colosseum at Liverpool, which expressed in the surpliced chorus that flanked the revolving stage where a Derby

THE OPENING OF THE COLISEUM

From the "Daily Graphic," Dec. 26, 1912

was run and Roman chariots raced on concentric circles, the faith of Stoll in the music-hall's higher destiny. When Stoll decided to direct a circuit of his own again, the Coliseum's huge profits showed how far-seeing he had been in his ambition to make variety scrupulously respectable and grand.

CHAPTER FOUR

Dan Leno—Marie Lloyd— Little Tich

WITH a quick, timid look over his shoulder into the wings to make sure he is *not being overheard*, the little figure in front of the scene of shops in a street so deserted that it seems always Sunday afternoon, takes all the hundreds of us completely into his confidence about family affairs. There is a perpetually startled look in his bright, merrily gleaming eyes, framed in semi-circular brows, and in his jerky movements; there is eagerness in every part of him from the disconcerting legs to the straight, strained mouth set in the curious double-rim formed by the lines of the cheeks. He wants to tell us his secrets. He must tell us. For the sake of his own peace of mind he wants to explain how he is related to somebody or other who has become involved in a scandal. "It's like this," he begins only to realise it is not so, for he has become thoroughly confused over his uncles, cousins, father and grandfathers. Then he pauses with his fingers over his mouth and suddenly croaks, "There's a postman mixed up in all this."

That was Dan Leno. In the midst of wildly fantastic fun, he would mutter some half-spoken thought like that and relate it all to reality. Then, as a critic said in a happy moment, "whole breadths of London rushed into view, all the flickering street corners on Saturday nights, all the world of crowded door-steps and open windows." In him cockney comedy came to full bloom. He created the humour of the humble home—the mockery of hardships, the laughter at squalor, the mirth over domestic drudgery, born of endurance. These jokes of desperation came naturally to him because he had experienced the miseries of poverty almost from the time of his birth in 1860 at a spot now covered by St. Pancras Station. His parents, whose real name was Galvin, were appearing at concerts as Mr. and Mrs. John Wilde. When his father died, his mother married a performer named William Grant whose stage name was Leno. The infant made his first public appearance at the age of four, as the partner of

31

his brother Jack. Next he had to perform with his uncle, Johnny Danvers, who was the elder by four weeks. Together these two children danced for hours in public-houses to earn a handful of coppers. If lucky, they were allowed to lie down on the bare boards of a garret afterwards—but not to sleep. According to Sir Seymour Hicks, who had the story from Leno himself, they then performed for one another's benefit. Each would tell the other stories. The one who made the other laugh got up from the floor, rolled up the blind as though it were an act-drop, and bowed to an imaginary audience on the tiles.

Forming a company of four with Dan's parents, they travelled round the country with an old iron bedstead as the apparatus of their turn. Each Sunday the two boys took this on to the stage to see that it could be well secured. One night they had to bore a hole to manage this, each in turn striking a match as a light for the other to work by. Presently they saw a gleam in the mezzanine below. Dan said, "We've set the theatre on fire," and Johnny emptied a bucket down the hole to put it out. Actually it was the lantern of the groom who was a feeding a pony, and as the water had dropped down his neck they had to run for their lives.

On page 33 is reproduced the bill of Pullan's Theatre of Varieties, Brunswick Place, Bradford, for Monday, May 20, 1878. The champion dancer, at the bottom of the bill in the smallest type, was having a hard time of it. He danced until there was hardly any sole left under his clogs. In 1880 he won a championship belt, and retained his title until a judgment was unfairly given against him. For some months after that he sang a libellous song describing how the belt had been stolen while he was executing the winning dance. In 1883 he won a handsome belt as champion clog dancer of the world after a six nights' contest against all-comers. When his youthful energy slackened he no longer danced, although he could casually take a stride of six feet or slap the sole of his shoe on the stage with a report like a pistol shot.

While Leno was touring the provinces, George Conquest heard his song, "Milk For Twins," and engaged him for two pantomimes at the old Surrey. There he caught the eye of Augustus Harris and went to Drury Lane, in 1888, as the Baroness in "The Babes In The Wood And Robin Hood And His Merry Men And Harlequin Who Killed Cock Robin." According to Hickory Wood, wittiest of pantomime authors, Dan Leno could be "quite a possible queen" when he chose, even though she lived under such conditions that a pair of braces was the natural thing to buy the king on his birthday, while the mistake of handing him a parcel of lingerie by mistake, to be opened in full view of the Court, was one that any royal lady might make. In his studies of women in a humble walk of life,

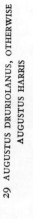

29 AUGUSTUS DRURIOLANUS, OTHERWISE
AUGUSTUS HARRIS

28 DAN LENO, JOHNNY DANVERS
AND HERBERT CAMPBELL
(Reading from top)

27 DAN LENO AS THE BEAUTIFIED
MOTHER GOOSE

30 A PANTOMIME POSTER OF DAN LENO

said Hickory Wood, Dan Leno's gait, manner and expression were altered, and all his dignity vanished :

He was homely, discursive and confidential, not to say occasionally aggressive. His own personality was, of course, ever present, but when I saw him playing this kind of parts, the impression he left on my mind was not so much a picture of Dan Leno playing the part of a woman in a particular walk of life as the picture of what Dan Leno would have been if he had been that particular woman.

Wash-tubs filled with tattered underwear, and kitchen tables loaded with a mess of uncooked, adhesive pastry, were not necessary to Dan Leno. As a designing Sister Anne, who wondered "did she push" herself too much, but tried all the same to capture the heart of Bluebeard with "When The Heart Is Young" until her hair got caught in the strings of her harp ; as Widow Twankey, making fatuous observations upon the tricks of the Slave of the Lamp (who was Cinquevalli) ; as Cinderella's stepmother mocking the flunkey who tried to stop her from coming to the ball, his humour was so closely related to real life that people who wanted pantomime to be really childish nonsense protested. Childish nonsense

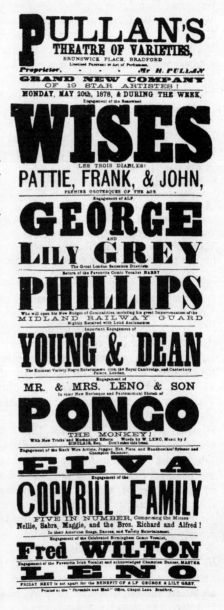

WHEN DAN LENO WAS BOTTOM OF
THE BILL

F

was what Dan Leno revelled in off the stage. When he learned that Whimsical Walker was expecting a dog by train, he entered the Clown's house in his absence, waited there with a box, abused Walker on his arrival for cruelty because the dog had not been given a drop of water, and swore that the R.S.P.C.A. should be informed. When Walker put his hand inside the box, he found the poor beast was stone cold. "It's dead, Dan," he said before he found it was a pantomime dog from the property-room.

Leno never rested. On and off the stage he *had* to make people laugh. There was a driving urgency about his jesting. We feel it when we recall his quick staccato style. You can sense it even now in the bare print of his patter :

Of course there are three kinds of Eggs—there is the new-laid Egg (that of course is nearly extinct) then there is the fresh Egg, that is almost the same as the new laid—but then comes *The* Egg, well, that is the Egg I'm talking about—that is the Egg that causes the trouble, a little round white thing. You can't tell what it is thinking about. You dare not kick it or drop it. It has got no face. You can't get it to laugh. No, you simply look at it and say : "Egg."

In the November of 1901 he sang "by command" before Edward VII at Sandringham. The honour was too much for him. There have been many attempts to describe how his mind snapped under the strain—how he gave away jewellery and money to odd strangers, how he raged against his friends one moment and begged their forgiveness the next, how his malady finally made itself known to all when he was seen capering near the stage-door of His Majesty's Theatre. The explanation of these seemingly disjointed episodes is given by Miss Constance Collier in *Harlequinade*. While acting at His Majesty's in "The Eternal City," she lived with her parents in Shaftesbury Avenue. Their little flat was at the top of a building. One night, on returning to it at about one o'clock, she and her mother happened to look into their sitting-room. There they saw, in "a little bit of moon under the window," Dan Leno. That was their first meeting. He had arrived two or three hours earlier and his brougham was still waiting outside. When he took her hand eagerly in a painful grip she felt he was trembling from excitement. With the moonlight on his face, for no one thought to light the gas, he "burst into his life story," saying that his father was a Scottish marquis and his mother a housemaid. "And then he told me the ambition of his life was to play Shakespeare"—Richard III and Hamlet.

Being advised by her to see Sir Herbert Tree at His Majesty's in the morning, he was happy when he went way, and at the theatre the next morning she found he had been there for about two hours, giving the stage-doorkeeper money to buy a silk hat; drawing up contracts for players in his Shakespearean company, and bestowing handfuls of money on newspaper boys, while a happy crowd looked on. The rehearsal of a curtain-raiser began. Miss Collier went through her part with Dan Leno constantly at her side until Tree entered and took him into the stalls. They talked there, "face to face, excitedly nodding and agreeing," until somebody was called to take charge of the poor little man.

On her return home that afternoon, she found him waiting there to offer her a diamond plaque, with a contract to be his leading lady. When she declined, as gently as she could, he left "with tears pouring down his face"—and on his way home gave the plaque to a barmaid. Just before the next Christmas he was well enough to join the panto-mime company at Drury Lane. The next year Miss Collier saw him at a music-hall, where he looked bewildered because the audience didn't laugh. "I wish he had never come back," she writes. "He died soon after." So little and frail a lantern, as Max Beerbohm wrote, "could not long harbour so big a flame."

*　*　*　*　*

Every generation elects a bad girl of the family. While she may be blameless in private, she must be (or thought to be) shameless in public. That explains why so many tongues are busy to-day making Mae West the heroine of stories told in other centuries of Peg Woffington and Nell Gwynn. Fifty years ago Bessie Bellwood was the heroine. When she died the public chose Marie Lloyd. All London's famous hussies have been well beloved, but none more than she. As long as music-halls are remembered, her name will be a legend.

That familiar story of how she sang to the licensing authorities indicates her style. In answer to a complaint from the unco' guid, she said the songs mentioned in the protest should be tested at a private hearing. Before a solemn audience, she sang each one "straight" without gesture or grimace. No fault could be found. When judg-ment had been passed in her favour, she sang one or two sentimental ballads in such a way that "every little movement had a meaning of its own." After this the committee might have been expected to reverse its decision. That they did nothing of the kind is over-whelming proof of "Marie's" power of making people realise how much more freedom should be given to the good-natured "bad girl" than to all the rest of the family put together. It is not easy to understand critics who spoke of her "vulgarity and coarseness." She was "of the people and for the people," happy when laughing

at the "would-be-if-they-could-be toffs," and surprised when Sarah
Bernhardt described her as "the one woman of genius on the English
stage." But there was delicacy in what was called her "indelicacy."

All the many scandalmongers, schoolboys and adults with schoolboy minds, who made her the heroine of exploits which were actually
performed by others, missed the secret of her success. She was not
another hoyden like Bessie Bellwood, without any sense of shame or
any pride in personal appearance. What was most typical of Marie
Lloyd expressed itself in every little movement of her plump, dainty
hands. All the sisters, as well as Marie Lloyd junior, have exquisite
fingers. They display them naturally and unaffectedly; but Marie
Lloyd wove with them a spell of magic. Coarseness? Vulgarity?
Critics who used such words must have been blind. Improper—yes.
But anyone who had eyes to see sat too enchanted to worry overmuch
about that.

Before leaving the subject of respectability, let me add a scrap of
history connected with it to prove how good-natured she could be.
Remember she did not shock people in order to gain notoriety,
play to the gallery, or increase the rush to the box-office. Out of a
thorough disgust with smug hypocrisy, she felt compelled to make
war on Mid-Victorianism. The imp of mischief possessed her so
that she never cared whether she went too far. She could—and did
—give performances which were quite fit for children to see, as some
who saw her at a seaside matinée will swear to. Yet rather than
promise to "tone down" her turn, she would forego any honours
or profits, and she was not included in the first Royal Variety Programme at the Palace in 1912. She threatened so forcibly to arrange
a Popular Demand programme as a rival show on the same night,
that she was taken seriously by those who did not know her well—
all of which adds to the significance of my scrap of history. Her
most persistent critic was one of her personal friends. His repeated
warnings in print against her offences against respectability led to
more forcible steps being taken. In reply she decided to quit the
halls and go on the stage. The play she chose was written by the
friend whose warnings had been the beginning of the squabble.
She knew he was honest and sincere, and that was all that mattered.

Her father was a waiter at the old Grecian Saloon, at the junction
of City Road and Shepherdess Walk in Shoreditch. His name
was Wood, and his nick-name "Brush" because he took the pride
in his personal appearance which she inherited. Matilda Alice Victoria
Wood, the eldest of his family of nine, was born on February 12,
1870. As the Grecian had become a theatre before then, and was
sold to the Salvation Army when she was eleven, you might wonder
how this spot could have been the nursery of her talent. Yet it was.

MARIE LLOYD.

WHIT MONDAY, 1893, DOUGLAS, ISLE OF MAN, FOR ONE MONTH. THEN STARRING PROVINCIAL TOUR UNTIL SEPT. 2.
LONDON, SEPTEMBER 4.

EASTER, 1893, CANTERBURY, EMPIRE, TROCADERO, OXFORD.

CHRISTMAS 1892-93, THEATRE ROYAL, DRURY LANE,
PRINCIPAL GIRL, RED RIDING HOOD.
SOLE AGENT, THE OLD RELIABLE, GEO. WARE.

FROM THE ENTR'ACTE ANNUAL OF 1892

37

Although General Booth owned the site, he was not empowered to pull down the Royal Eagle Tavern which was part of the property, and willy-nilly he had to let it continue as a house of drink and song. It was on Salvation Army ground, under the banner of "Blood And Fire," that Matilda Alice Victoria studied her impudent art. A lively account of how she prepared for this appeared under her name in a sixpenny pamphlet, published about 1896. To prove how much better her singing and dancing were than anything on the stage,

I would get all my young sisters, even the last baby sister, to go down into the coal-cellar or up to the back attic, and have them witness my grand and expert gyrations, and listen to my beautiful voice. It must have been beautiful, for every time I sang they would all try to join in with a sort of very primitive and somewhat noisy chorus, in which their yells would denote that they also possessed voices, probably not so sweet and beautiful as mine, but voices and lungs just the same. Even our blessed kid of six months old would join in and howl with delight, at least, I always imagined it was delight till my mother would come down to the cellar or up to the attic and sternly ask me what I was doing with the poor baby.

Supposing Matilda was then at the age of ten, her audience would have consisted of her brother John, aged nine, and four sisters. Alice Lloyd was then seven years old, Grace (Alice's partner in the Lloyd Sisters turn) five years, and Daisy Wood, three years, with Rosie Lloyd as the howling baby of six months. Their applause helped the budding genius to make up her mind, especially after she had successfully organised her school friends into "The Fairy Bell Minstrels," and after she had made her first solo appearance in public with "Throw Down The Bottle And Never Drink Again," at a Band of Hope concert. Through her father's help she was given her first chance when "little over fourteen years of age."

As the accounts of this are conflicting, I have consulted Mr. John Parker, editor of Who's Who in the Theatre, who had the facts from Marie Lloyd herself. General Booth's Royal Eagle Music Hall (not the Eagle in Mile End Road which had been burned down and rebuilt as the Paragon), was more than a mere tavern sing-song. Jenny Hill, Alice Leamar (now living at Brinsworth among other veterans of variety), and Herbert Campbell, were there during that first week of May, 1885, when (on the Saturday night, May 9) Matilda Alice Victoria Wood was added to the bill as an extra turn, under the name of Bella Delmere. In later years she told Mr. Parker that her songs were "My Soldier Laddie" and "Time Is Flying." He found the name of Marie Lloyd in print for the first time at the Royal Eagle on June 22 that year.

The next year she sang at the Falstaff, Old Street, and Belmont's

Sebright Music Hall, next at the Star, Bermondsey, where her songs were "And The Leaves Began To Fall," "Sure To Fetch Them," "Harry's A Soldier," and "She Has A Sailor For A Lover." From the Bedford, Camden Town, she went to the Old Mo, in Drury Lane, with Nelly Power's song "The Boy I Love Sits Up In The Gallery." She at once became a public idol. She was engaged at the Oxford for a year without a break, and might have continued longer had not Augustus Harris, having quarrelled with the Vokes family of dancers who had been the mainstay of pantomime at Drury Lane, looked to the music-halls to replace them and chose her for his principal girl. According to Arthur Roberts, she asked, when they met at lunch, "What theatre did you say?"

"Drury Lane," boomed Gus Harris, with a note of astonishment in his voice, "Drury Lane, my girl."

"Oh, but I have been playing at the Middlesex already in Drury Lane."

THE MIDDLESEX

DRURY LANE.

PROPRIETOR AND MANAGER. ... ... MR. J. L. GRAYDON

J. L. GRAYDON

Begs to announce that the

MIDDLESEX ANNIVERSARY

Will take place on

Thursday, November 20th, 1902.

A GALAXY OF STARS! | GRAND FLORAL DISPLAY.

The following Artistes have consented to appear by kind permission of their respective Managers

"OUR MARIE"
The Popular and only

MARIE LLOYD

WHO WILL SING SOME OF HER VERY LATEST SUCCESSES

Nat Clifford	Emmie Ames	Phil Sinclair
Edisonograph	Mabel Toney	Cliff Ryland
Sam Mayo	Chas. Wood	Joe Mac
Caselli Sisters	Flo Melville	Lily Langtry
W. H. Downes	Kavades	Ella Lane
Phillips and Terry	La Tostia	Eva Searle
Frank Seeley	Dante and Elton	Walter Stanley
Alice Lloyd	Ray and Calden	Herbert Le Martine
Marguerite Broadfoote	Walter King	Lulu Gould

DATAS

HERBERT CAMPBELL | MAGGIE DUGGAN

Heeley and Meeley	The Two Graces	Dot Carey
Lydia Dudley	Tally-Ho-Trio	Bessie Butt
Pat Carey	Dale and O'Malley	The Korries
Dora Lyric	Amy Clevere	Kitty Clover & Co.,

GEO. D'ALBERT | VESTA VICTORIA

R. W. Bentley	Queenie Lawrence	Master Cliff
Rich and Rich	The 4 Eldorados	Alexandre & Hughes
Hy. Bancroft	Maud Mortimer	Floradora Girls
Lilian Lea	Victor Travers	Millie Denham
Condon and Preston	R. H. Douglas	Charles Gardiner

CLARA WIELAND | BELLA AND BIJOU

George Gilbey	Sisters Swinson	Vera Vere
Pueblo Bros	May Moore Duprez	Maud Dewey
Fred Langton	Hudson Banjo Trio	Sisters Lyan
Arthur Rigby	Albert Whelan	Unthan

THE TWO McNAUGHTONS

Childie Stuart	Primavesi	Ella and Rose
Maud Beaumont	Drew and Alders	Sisters Morde
Harry Pleon.	Harry Trevor	Gus Hindell

ARTHUR REECE | GEO. MOZART

Charles Austin	Sid Ryhart	Tom Stuart
The New Macs	Harry Tate	Harry Maxam
The 6 Gatlings	Pat Rafferty	George Bendon
Will Newman	Tom Yorke	The Kellys
Henry Moore	Bros. Donar	Marvellous Frank
Edgar Granville	Nellie Farrell	Ryan

THE WORLD RENOWNED

BOISSET TROUPE

IN "THE WILD WEST."

MUSICAL DIRECTOR ... ... MR. LESLIE SMITH

Prices of Admission. 5s., 2s.6d., 1s., 9d., and 6d.
OPEN AT 6. COMMENCE AT 6-30.

A. MANSON, Printer, Fleet Street, Drury Lane

STAR OF A "GALAXY OF STARS"

replied Marie with the straightest and simplest of faces. "Do you want me to go back there?"

In an endeavour to explain that he was not referring to the Old Mo, but to the great Theatre Royal, Harris described how it was (in those days) guarded day and night by sentries drawn from the Grenadier and Coldstream Guards. "A sort of light" seemed to break on Marie's mind:

"Oh, do you mean that horrible-looking place," she said, "which stands at the end of the Lane with the soldiers round it? Why, I always thought that place was the prison! Still, I'll go there if you pay me enough."

Actually, "she felt the proudest little woman in the world," on joining the brilliant band at Old Drury, with Dan Leno, Herbert Campbell and Little Tich. One year she was Princess Allfair in "Humpty-Dumpty," the next Red Riding Hood in "Little Bo-Peep," and the next Polly in "Robinson Crusoe," pantomimes which ran from Boxing Day until Quarter Day in March. But the critics were not pleased. William Archer, by no means the severest, complained:

Nothing, apparently, can subdue Mr. Dan Leno, who appeared as Crusoe's mother. The most successful incident of the evening was the bedroom scene, in which Miss Marie Lloyd modestly disrobed and retired to rest. At every string she untied, the gallery gave a gasp of satisfaction; and when Mr. Dan Leno exhibited himself in a red flannel petticoat and pair of stays, the whole house literally yelled with delight. You may think it odd, and even ungallant, but somehow I don't seem to yearn for the privilege of assisting at Miss Marie Lloyd's toilet, or admiring Mr. Dan Leno in *déshabille*; but amid all that vast audience, I was evidently in a minority of one.

She was married to Percy Courtney at seventeen. There was a divorce in 1904 and she became the wife of Alec Hurley, "the coster king," who died in 1913. Her third husband was Bernard Dillon, the jockey.

Off the stage she had to face many misfortunes, yet she was never embittered. Her gaiety on the stage was the true expression of her recklessly good-natured character. All the fortunes she made while touring the British Isles, the United States, Canada, South Africa and Australia, were distributed among needy friends and acquaintances. Whether in sickness or in health she continued to sing in order to provide for the large number of her pensioners and also to pay life insurance premiums so that she should leave a large sum at her death no matter how poor she might be in life. In the hope of peaceful

31 and 32 *A song-front portrait of* MARIE LLOYD *and an Entr'acte caricature showing General Booth as landlord of the Eagle Tavern at the time she began life there, while* GEORGE CONQUEST, *who formerly ran it with the Grecian Saloon, considers "I may be wanted back yet."*

33 MARIE LLOYD WITH HER SECOND HUSBAND, ALEC HURLEY

From a photograph taken at Adelaide
during their Australian tour of 1901

years of retirement, she bought a public house in the West End but had to give it up two years later, and return, although her health was failing, to the halls. One happy event relieved the heavy labour of those last years. The public did not need reminding that February 12, 1920, was her fiftieth birthday. Many came to the Bedford Music Hall that night with gifts. The stage looked like a flower-show.

MUSIC HALL WAR.

Mr. Gibbons says his companies consist of picked artistes and musicians.

Mr. JOE ELVIN says:

Unfortunately, he picked them before they were ripe!

DOWN WITH THE TRUSTS!

ONE OF THE HAND-BILLS DISTRIBUTED BY VARIETY ARTISTES' FEDERATION
PICKETS AT THE DOORS OF WEST END MUSIC-HALLS IN JANUARY, 1907

Arthur Roberts, Joe Elvin, and other veterans of variety, appeared on the stage to present her with a bouquet from which a bottle of champagne was hanging. She was excited with delight, and then she collapsed.

Despite increasing illness, she continued to sing frequently. She was so weak that her totterings and staggerings which excited laughter when she sang "One Of The Ruins That Cromwell Knocked About A Bit," were unfeigned, as the audience realised when a weary, grey-haired ageing woman came before the curtain to return thanks. She struggled on until the beginning of October, 1922. One night it was impossible for her to leave her home. Three nights later, on October 7, she was dead. She possessed less than a week's salary

G

for herself. But she left £7000, which was typical of her instinctive self-sacrifice.

★　★　★　★　★

At his birth there was laughter. The whole parish of Cudham, near Sevenoaks, that summer of 1868, joked about the quizzical look of Mrs. Relph's new baby. She had him christened "Harry" but the neighbours found another name for him. Those were the days of the celebrated Tichborne trial, and as the claimant to the title was stout, there was a general tendency to call any fat person after him. So at Cudham, Harry Relph was always known as the Little Tichborne. In time this became Little Tich for short. As such he laid his claim to Fame and as such the smallest of comedians became well-known the world over for many years before his death in 1928. He has left memories that are a living part of us. Without as much as closing your eyes you may see again that imp who represented the life of London's thoroughfares under the diminishing glass. Here they are, the grocer, the butcher's boy, the sailor on leave, the blacksmith, the chorus girl, and the dandy with six huge buttons on his coat and a cane to flick nonchalantly.

Probably what decided his career was his parents' decision to move house to Gravesend. Rosherville, practically the last of the old pleasure gardens where Londoners had revelled for a couple of centuries, was there, and one of the singers at its concerts was a schoolboy. Harry Relph, determined to outdo him, studied in secret how to play the tin whistle. With this additional accomplishment he presented himself to the manager and was "taken on." So great was his success that in a very short time he was earning as much as threepence a song.

In his teens he obtained engagements at London music-halls and a Glasgow pantomime. At that time he was a black-faced entertainer with song and dance. As such he went to America, but there he found that nigger minstrels were out of favour. While with a company which acted burlesques at the Chicago Opera House, he washed his face and stayed washed on his return to England in a Manchester pantomime. During the music-hall invasion of Drury Lane, he played Hop o' My Thumb, then Humpty-Dumpty, and next Man Friday—his face still stayed washed even for this part. There was trouble during the run of "Robinson Crusoe." As Polly, Marie Lloyd sang a song called "A Saucy Bit O' Crackling" which shocked the critics. Reform was demanded; and Augustus jumped at the chance to cut his huge expenses. Though Dan Leno was guilty, he was not told to go. Little Tich, without offending, was "thrown to the wolves of criticism."

From music-hall to music-hall, from city to city, from country to country the world over, Little Tich now toured with ever-growing success. In Paris he was made an officer of the French Academy. Sacha Guitry, and such leading critics as Gustave Fréjaville, regarded him as a "classic." But in Australia some twelve months or so before he died, his tour was so disappointing that he all but broke down. Audiences who little understood the tradition he represented would have none of him. Of course, Little Tich at the age of 59 was not as magnetic as he was when we were very young. For several years he had not donned those extraordinary boots, as long as he was high, for the sand dance. If you never saw Little Tich perform this, you can have no idea of his powers. Although once the stock-in-trade of comedians, it was never so surprising as when he sprang into the air, balancing himself on the tips of those elongated soles that stood up like stilts.

In his thumbnail sketches of tradesmen he re-awakened our child-hood's wonder at things grown-ups find humdrum. Not since the days we clung to our mothers' skirts were we aware that shops were full of smells. As our noses have grown farther from the floor and even from the counter, while our lives and minds have moved away from the trembling scales, we have forgotten the thrill of these. But the excitement came back directly Little Tich put on the apron and whiskers of the grocer. The ozone of tea, sawdust, soap, coffee, cheese, bacon, "improper prunes," blue paper, and new packages —heavy in the layer of air swirled about by bustling feet and trodden-on lap-dogs—could be sniffed again as in the hours when we privily decided to go straight home and "play shops."

We never saw such a grocer. But all the grocers of our childhood strove, like this little fellow, to be "affability itself." Although they did not lie on the floor and howl with the enjoyment of their puns while an unappreciative customer walked off with "two scrubbing brushes and three bars of soap," they did rub their hands and try to be bright about the nice brightness of the mornings; and the impression their words made on our minds could only be duplicated in later years by the implacable humour of Little Tich when he replied to the question, "Why does tea leave tea-leaves when it leaves?" with "Because the coffee has been a bean before it has been a has-been." Memory's *pot-pourri* withered as he strutted away. When he returned as "Just Presented At Court," he brought us face to face with that acute problem of adult life, feminine self-deception. We foresaw how the imaginary admiral—"that full-faced man sucking an orange in the corner over there"—would suffer through saying he wanted to meet this nightmare of determined and inappropriate coyness.

Dislocated romance also inspired his Queen of the Fairies. Into a country garden, full of trim box-hedges and masses of red roses, tripped a figure that might almost have been fairy-like and dainty. The garland round the auburn hair was entrancing, and so was the pleated skirt, flowing out on either side to resemble wings. But the legs underneath the skirt were knobbly and the nose beneath the wig red. At moments he flitted with grace and ease, at other times he came a cropper : all his horseplay did not always bar a fleeting incongruous hint of a dancer's swift beauty from escaping occasionally.

Life's little worries were studied by Little Tich with the zeal of a butterfly collector. Each specimen of a fall or trip specially calculated to annoy was caught in his net and preserved. Some occurred in the life of his blacksmith, who bravely swung his hammer until it swung against his foot, so that the implement wielded to express health and strength had next to support him as a crutch. As a sailor, troubled severely by sea-sickness, he drove despair away with a hornpipe. So long as he danced, troubles were forgotten : but his particular misfortune was his trousers' tendency to "carry too much sail," and slip down whenever he made any very carefree movement.

You remember his juggling ? "Very difficult," he said, by way of preface. He attempted the trick and failed ; tried again and failed. Then he said, "Too difficult." It was the clue to his philosophy, this jest at tribulation. That was on the stage. He rarely saw the jest off the stage. He was painfully conscious of his physical peculiarities, of the freakish extra finger on each of his hands. Nor was he happy in exciting laughter. He wanted higher tribute than that. He wanted to be praised for his art, to be taken seriously—a desire not altogether unlike Leno's ambition to play Hamlet.

LITTLE TICH AS MAN FRIDAY
According to the Drury Lane "book of words," 1893-4

34 LITTLE TICH. HIS SAND-DANCE SHOES IN THIS COSTUME ARE NOT THE
YARD-LONG ONES HE WORE FOR HIS ACROBATICS

35 CONNIE GILCHRIST (THE COUNTESS OF ORKNEY)

CHAPTER FIVE

"Direct from Drury Lane"

WHAT *caused* our English Christmas pantomime? How did fairy tales and nursery rhymes get mixed up with music-hall turns, patriotic tableaux, topical allusions, transformation scenes, tradesmen's advertisements, actresses in thigh boots and comedians in petticoats, fairy queens with love songs, and fire fiends with songs about storms at sea? And why is such a talkative mixture given a name that means, at all other seasons except Christmas, *dumbshow*?

Out of a jumble of explanations, we must fasten on the clue that pantomime was never invented. It grew, early in the eighteenth century, out of dances by harlequins that were inserted in any play, tragedy, or comedy, and also into a mixture of opera and ballet, described as "after the fashion of the ancient pantomimes" because the plots were taken from the fables of Rome and Greece. Although these ballet-operas soon went out of fashion, their name of "pantomime" became the label, through confusion of thought, for any entertainment as long as Harlequin and Columbine eloped in it, pursued by Clown and Pantaloon. Such harlequinade-pantomimes were, throughout the eighteenth century, the brief "after-pieces" of performances for adults in spring, summer, autumn or winter. When they became Christmas entertainments for children, nursery heroes and heroines took the places once occupied by pagan gods and goddesses. Nowadays, when Harlequin and Columbine are only permitted to flit on and off for old time's sake, their love scenes are acted by principal boy and principal girl.

Why have actresses to play heroes? People still ask the question. That funny men should dress up as old women is taken for granted since it has been a recognised joke for centuries. That handsome girls should make a deliberately ineffectual pretence of being heroic young men, is not nearly so old an idea. In the plays, novels and poems of Shakespeare's day, heroines often disguise themselves in the doublet and hose that principal boys wear in Act I at Christmas now, but they always began in skirts and ended in skirts. There was a difference in the "male impersonations" of Peg Woffington, for she took parts written for actors. The next development was a fashion to present actresses as the heroes

H

in opera. From that to burlesque and thence to pantomime were easy stages.

Consequently, when the Christmas revels of the theatre ceased to be performed by actors and actresses (some seventy years ago) and were entrusted to music-hall folk instead, the *serio comic* with her "acres of tights," swaggering stride and glittering, beribboned silver-topped staff, was naturally engaged for Prince Charming, Dick Whittington, Aladdin and the rest of those gallant youths whose ability to win hearts and fortunes gave us, in the nursery, a feeling of inferiority nothing in after life has been able to remove. Round about the time Harriet Vernon was in full bloom, the players of these parts would *recline* (the very word has now gone out of fashion) sumptuously in feather-beds every morning and early afternoon until the call-boy began to sing his matinée song of "Overture-beginners— please." All the exercise they took was to toss aside, unread, the notes from vast bouquets of mutely and vainly appealing roses from Guardsmen and foreign noblemen. Tireless maids helped them into seas of petticoats, and muscular dressers helped them to emerge from these when they at length arrived at the theatre. Then the real business of lacing began, calling for the utmost exertions of maids and dressers combined. I remember a doctor had to be called because a girl had fainted during this tussle with corsets. He asked for the principal boy, but she was none the worse. The casualty was one of the maids who had been tugging.

To tell the story of Herbert Campbell is to describe Drury Lane pantomime throughout its most exciting years. No other comedian can equal his record; he was regularly engaged there, from the Boxing Night of 1882 to the early spring of 1904, in over a score of the most celebrated pantomimes ever staged. Many famous people played leading parts in the comedies and tragedies that formed the highly-coloured background of his life. Clowns mingle with countesses in that strange panorama which reveals all the peculiar romance of London Society from the zenith of Queen Victoria's reign to its close.

During the Nigger Minstrel boom, a burnt-cork trio known as Harman, Campbell and Elston became popular until the middle man, deciding that it was a pity to cover his broad jolly face with burnt cork, broke away and became a solo turn on the halls, and Harry Nicholls' partner in pantomimes at the Grecian. When he made his Drury Lane début in 1882, he was thirty-eight, so that he was from the start the eldest of that merry band although he remained longer than any other. That year Nellie Power was "Sindbad" (correctly spelt with two "d's" in those days) and Vesta Tilley was Captain Tralala.

For the next five years Herbert Campbell and Harry Nicholls provided most of the "comedy" between them. In one of those pantomimes Connie Gilchrist, who began as a skipping-rope dancer

FISH BALLET DESIGNS FROM THE BOOK OF WORDS OF "ROBINSON CRUSOE," DRURY LANE, 1893-4

on the halls, played the last part of her brief though famous career, as a magician in "The Forty Thieves" a few years before she became the Countess of Orkney, leaving playgoers a legacy of fragrant memories. The judge who asked "Who is Connie Gilchrist?" was laughed at throughout the country; and the young townsman, showing his country cousin the sights from the top of a horse-bus and hesitating what to tell her about the statue to Queen Anne in St. Paul's Churchyard, was enjoined by the driver, "Come on, guv'nor, don't give in. Tell 'er it's Connie Gilchrist."

When Herbert Campbell and Harry Nicholls were the Babes in the Wood for the season of 1888-9, there was a magnificent Robin Hood, for Harriet Vernon was the statuesque principal boy. There was also a diminutive dame, for the Wicked Aunt was played by Dan Leno on his first appearance at Old Drury. The next year, Augustus Harris saw the possibilities of a close partnership between the largest and smallest of his comedians. Herbert Campbell was Queen Fanny the Flirt in "Jack And The Beanstalk," with Dan Leno as Mrs. Simpson, her best friend. Harry Nicholls was still there as the King.

Comic relief was not the mainstay of the following pantomime, for Harris had planned to exploit a society scandal into a stage sensation. All the world knew about the romantic marriage of Belle Bilton. When singing with her sister on the halls as the Sisters Bilton, she had won the heart of Lord Dunlo, both at twenty years of age. There had been a secret ceremony and a quiet honeymoon at a hotel in Northumberland Avenue before the Earl of Clancarty brought such pressure to bear that the bridegroom set out for Australia only nine days after the wedding. "I love you dearly," he wrote to his wife, but on his return he was persuaded by his father to sign a petition for divorce. Directly the case was heard he declared his belief in her innocence so firmly that there was applause in court and outside.

"Druriolanus" saw his chance. With a sudden change of plans he chose "Beauty And The Beast" as the subject of his pantomime for the Christmas of 1890, and announced that Lady Dunlo would be Beauty, leaving the public to guess whether any reference to her husband's "change of face" was intended by the story of a hero temporarily changed into a beast. She returned to her old life so simply and naturally that Whimsical Walker (so that fine old clown told me) often sat by her side while they dined at the bar of a ham-and-beef shop. When the nine days' wonder died, Lady Dunlo was not such a great success as had been expected and her engagement ended when she was slightly hurt in an accident—a few months before her persecutor died and she left the stage to become Lady Clancarty.

Meanwhile Harris had offended Vesta Tilley whom he had originally asked to appear at Drury Lane that season as Dick Whittington. After agreeing to play King Courage instead, she found at rehearsal that from the second scene to the finale the hero had to appear masked, and insisted that John d'Auban, the stage-manager, should represent the Beast. That left her free to accept variety engagements, through-

37 FLO BILTON

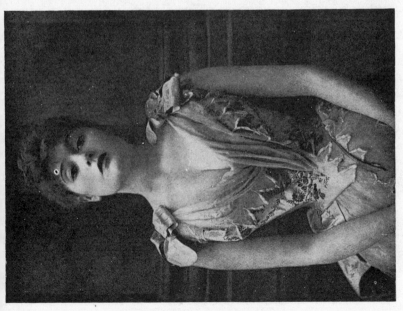

36 BELLE BILTON (LADY DUNLO)

38 HERBERT CAMPBELL AS "BERTIE THE MASHER"

From a coloured song-front

out the run, which trebled her salary. She "never quite forgave Harris," and refused to act at Drury Lane any more.

Whatever principal boys and principal girls might come and go,

MORE FISH FROM THE BALLET IN THE DRURY LANE PANTOMIME OF 1893-4

Campbell and Leno seemed likely to go on for ever—to the satisfaction of everybody save Bernard Shaw:

I hope I may never again have to endure anything more dismally futile than the efforts of Mr. Leno and Mr. Herbert Campbell to start a passable

"DIRECT FROM DRURY LANE"

---

joke in the course of their stumblings and wanderings through barren acres of gag on Boxing Night. Their attempt at a travesty of *Hamlet* reached a pitch of abject resourcelessness which could not have been surpassed if they really had been a couple of school children called on for a prize-day Shakespearean recitation without any previous warning.

In spite of this they still continued the mainstay of pantomime; they were also often together on the halls. The Tivoli programme for the week ending April 15, 1893, numbers them among twenty-six turns (counting the "Overture" but no "Intermission") with Arthur Rigby, Harry Freeman, Florence Levey, George Robey, Tom Costello, Harriet Vernon, Eugene Stratton, James Fawn, Bessie Bellwood, Harry Randall, George Beauchamp and Albert Chevalier —practically all at the height of their popularity. That Saturday night Herbert Campbell had a new macintosh. While he was making up, according to a tale Harry Randall tells in his biography, Dan Leno came out of the little ante-room where they hung their coats and presented each of them with a square of the macintosh, which he had cut into bits, remarking, "A little souvenir, with Herbert Campbell's compliments, on his departure from London."

In "Humpty-Dumpty," during the early months of 1904, they wound up with a verse announcing their resolve to return to Drury Lane each year for a long time to come. That was their last pantomime. Herbert Campbell died the next July (four months before Dan Leno), mourned by thousands who lined the funeral route from his house off Essex Road to Abney Park Cemetery.

* * * * *

What is the strange feeling which disturbs us when we think of our old favourites of Drury Lane pantomime? Mingled with our sorrow that so many of them are gone, are the lively excitements of Boxing Days many years ago. These sensations stirred in us in the spring of 1932 when we heard of the death, at the age of 72, of Harry Randall—the cook, when Dan Leno, in his last pantomime, was the Queen in "Humpty-Dumpty"—and they stir in us again whenever we read *Harry Randall, Old Time Comedian, by Himself*, for it seems to bring us in close contact with many an idol of our early Christmas holidays.

The funny man often starts out in an unfunny way. Harry Randall's was a particularly strange metamorphosis. As a "Heraldic artist and stone seal engraver," he had built up a profitable business which he was loth to sell. Fame was thrust upon him. At a very early age he had played in pantomime called, "Little Dicky Dilver With His Stock Of Silver; or, Harlequin Pretty Prince Pretty-Boy,

And The Three Comical Kings." In the animal kingdom scene he
had been a dog, in the vegetable scene a turnip, and in the mineral
kingdom a nugget of tin. This production was preceded by a
nautical drama with the great Phelps as hero, in which Master Randall
had to represent the captain of a steamer seen at a distance. All this
counted merely as a boyish escapade. Afterwards Randall gave up
the stage, so he thought, for good.

What brought him back to the footlights was his fondness for
"three-cornered puffs." They were offered to anyone who would
get up and sing at Saturday night concerts in a "teetotal hall."
Amateurs were busying themselves in every well-populated district
of the land. The barber supplied the music. He would "loan you
a published copy of the latest comic song for two hours for the price
of threepence and a two-bob deposit." By making copies, the performer could add to his repertoire at threepence a time. "Funny
men" needed costumes as well, and special business was done in these
at Petticoat Lane. The stall which specialised in supplying their
wants was run by "Mo" Harris, who welcomed them with "Hullo,
me lads ! Come for some funny stuff? Look at that—isn't it a
scream? You've only got to pop your nose on and they'll yell, and
'arf a mo', I've got a 'at 'ere. Funny? Why, you 'aven't got to
open yer mouth."

In Harry Randall's description of "Mo" there is a Dickens touch.
Young hopefuls of the Saturday night concerts found him a friendly
soul ; he was offended if they did not haggle with him over prices ;
and when the bargain was struck he took them home for refreshment.
He lived in one room. It had a big bedstead in the corner, with three
feather-beds piled on it. His wife, sitting beside a roaring fire, was
almost large enough to fill the one gap left by his goods :

A piano in one corner, with an antique brass fender and dogs on the top ;
officers' uniforms hung on nails ; umbrellas, walking sticks, gun cases, filling
up all the corners ; the mantelpiece piled with clocks, bronzes, and china—
other available spaces heaped up with second-hand theatrical dresses, and
an enormous table in the middle of the room crowded with bric-à-brac.

As the business of seal engraving was improving rapidly, Harry
Randall resolved to stay in it and refused an offer from Deacon's.
Not until his wife said, "If it were me, I wouldn't be told I was
afraid," did he consent. As last turn, he won prolonged applause.
Henceforth he was numbered among that merry throng of comedians,
buffo vocalists and *serio comics*, whose names are now legendary.
Off the stage they formed a friendly community, especially when
they met for a last drink, after the fall of all the curtains, at the long
bar of the Canterbury, while their broughams waited outside. One

lesser light, who owned a milk shop, drove up in his roundsman's chariot, but fame has not worried about him.

While playing Mrs. Sinbad at Drury Lane in the pantomime of 1906-7, Harry Randall took tea in a scene with Fred Emney, who stepped straight out of his character as Empress of all the Saharas to draw the realistic portrait of an "old geyser." That scene became the basis of "A Sister To Assist 'Er," a sketch in which Emney toured the halls for several years afterwards. On the opening night of "Cinderella" at the London Opera House in 1917, he joined in the knockabout "business" by sliding on the soap-suds slopped on the stage. But the fall that excited shouts of laughter was fatal. Internal injuries caused his death a few days later.

In "Sinbad" the Empress was courted by Harry Fragson, an Envoy with an incongruous grand piano which he played as he sang, "Billee, Billee Brown Of London." Because of his natural Cockney accent Fragson was as popular in Paris as he was, because of his cultivated French accent, in London. Though he led a merry life, he took loving care of his father—growing insane and jealous of his son's acquaintances—until it was necessary to arrange for the poor old man to be sent away to a house where he could be constantly attended. They were to separate on the last day of 1913. Two days before the New Year's Eve, in their home in Paris, the father waited with a loaded revolver for his son's return to change in readiness for his performance at the Alhambra, after dining with the woman he loved. She went to the station to meet one of his friends from England. To that chance she probably owed her life. Fragson was killed.

★   ★   ★   ★   ★

Who will ever forget Will Evans' hammer-headed nose, those gimlet eyes lit up by some intense fire of inward enjoyment, and the thin red line of that long mouth with vertically upturned slits at the corners? In the golden days of his clowning, Will Evans was the funniest comedian of the London stage. He proved it during the nights of the air-raids. I remember one such deserted evening in London. The lifeless, unlit streets were bright under a round, yellow moon. In the dead silence of Trafalgar Square the Australians, each with a "flapper," had taken seats on the parapets to be sure of seeing the Zeppelins. At the Empire there were barely fifty people in front. Yet on the stage there was mirth enough for a Boxing Night in peace time. The happiest scene represented a picnic in Leicester Square, with Will Evans as host. While he was engaged with a ripe camembert, Blanche Tomlin approached as a starving beggar-maid.

"Sing us a song," he said, "and you shall have a piece of this."

39 WILL EVANS

40 WILKIE BARD

Song-fronts reproduced by kind permission of Messrs. Francis, Day and Hunter

41 A DOUBLE-CROWN POSTER OF HARRY RANDALL

She sang. At first he munched his bread unconcernedly. Then the tune attracted him. He looked up still munching, and tears gradually filled his eyes. There was nothing more in the jest than that, for both he and the camembert remained still for the rest of the

THE REDECORATED CANTERBURY
From the "Daily Graphic," July 31, 1890

song. Yet the small scattered audience laughed at that process of mournful mastication until the house was filled with mirth.

With his passing, in the April of 1931, a link was broken in almost a century of laughter. Old Fred Evans, his father, was a worthy upholder of Grimaldi traditions in the harlequinade. Will Evans was born in London on May 29, 1875, and began his stage career in pantomime when Fanny Leslie played Robinson Crusoe and Arthur Roberts was Mrs. Crusoe, by appearing as an animal on the island, and taking part in the harlequinade, directed by his father as well. His peculiar bent was for those displays of bungling, which soon became a rage. They originated in the kitchen scenes of pantomime. Some humble job of work had to be performed in as hopeless and merry a manner as possible. Many comedians tried their hand at it, and the act became cut and dried. He was more amusing than the others because of his face. When he had finished slopping paste over the stage, himself and his companions, he would sit down to eat bread and cheese in such a state of crumby satisfaction with the whole of existence that we caught the infection of his zest and enjoyed life, too.

After playing Potterini in "Hop O' My Thumb" at Drury Lane at Christmas, 1911, he appeared as Pompos for three seasons—in "The Sleeping Beauty," "The Sleeping Beauty Reawakened," and "The Sleeping Beauty Beautified." Next he played the Grand Duke in "Puss In Boots" when the Grand Duchess was George Graves, who declares in his book, *Gaieties and Gravities*, that Will Evans' supreme gift was "consuming eggs," round about the time when London's favourite joke was the stockbroker who travelled to the City with egg stains on his moustache, and was accused—eggs being the price they were during the food shortage—of "Swank":

He came over to my room and chatted cheerfully in his simple-souled way and seemed quite unconcerned about the War situation, which, I confess, had got on the edge of my nerves. At last I pushed a map of the battle under his nose and said:

"Good God, Bill, look at this! It's only a question of hours before our Army look like being rolled up and pushed into the sea."

Will looked at the map and then at me and said:

"Oh, cheer up, George. Come over to my room and have an egg."

Later Will Evans turned playwright. "Tons Of Money," of which he was part author, ran for over seven hundred performances in 1922 and was revived ten years later. He grew rich on royalties. He grew contented with his lot, and the *vis comica* left him. When he returned to the stage, as one of the Ugly Sisters in "Cinderella" at the Scala, he had even discarded his famous hammer-headed nose, and was depressingly unfunny.

*　　*　　*　　*　　*

Amorous rascals, confiding dupes, expansive dowagers and wistfully argumentative old geysers are some of the types that suit Wilkie Bard's quiet, matter-of-fact manner best. That hiccuping sententiousness of his, with bland look and blinking eyes, has been imitated all over the world since, as mere Billie Smith, he amused his fellow-workers in a cotton-spinner's warehouse. He was born in Manchester, educated in Manchester, employed in Manchester, and given his first chance at the Slip Inn, Manchester.

His first professional engagement was on February 11, 1895, when he was under twenty-one, at the Grand, Manchester. He appeared as a coster singer with "'E Ain't The Bloke I Took 'Im For At All," and "Never 'Ave A Lodger For A Pal." A month later he was at Collins's, Islington Green, where he persuaded even the audiences from Hoxton and Shoreditch to accept him as the singer in character of "All Becos 'E's Minding A 'Ouse."

It was when he adopted the high, bald forehead of the Bard that he became famous. The addition of large black spots over the eyes, gave further distinction to the portrait. That is how he has appeared in a score of both male and female disguises. There is "The Turkish Bath Attendant" who makes the thermometer rise by flirting with the barmaid. There is the prima donna who announces in "The Beauty Parlour" that she's "coming back," and is asked, "What, are you *going*?" There is the salesman in "The Boot Shop" who destroys a £20 note to save his beautiful customer from being arrested as a counterfeiter by a detective—only to discover after he has had to make it good in cash that both are crooks. There is also "The Park Keeper" who is nothing if not human. The golfer with a gun hidden amongst his golf clubs may shoot what rabbits and windows he likes—after he has parted with pound notes and uncorked his flask. And for the sake of the nurse who shares his seat, the keeper is ready to lock the gates before the time appointed—only to find that her husband has already entered the park.

During his pantomime career, Wilkie Bard has twice appeared at Drury Lane—as Idle Jack in the "Dick Whittington" of Christmas 1908, when he started the vogue of tongue-twister songs with "She Sells Sea-Shells On The Sea-Shore," and as Widow Twankey in "Aladdin" the next year.

*   *   *   *   *

Where is Johnny Danvers now? Our good friend of Drury Lane pantomimes, the singer of "I've Got The Ooperzootic" is an old favourite we have missed of late. Like his nephew, Dan Leno, he belonged to the 1860 vintage. Their boyhood was spent together, but they began many miles apart, for while Dan Leno was a Cockney, Johnny was born and educated in Yorkshire, and made his first appearance as a boy at the Alexandra, Sheffield. For many years he shared the heartache, poverty and hardships of the Leno family on the road, and was engaged by Conquest to play Silly Billy in "Robinson

Crusoe" at the Surrey, still accompanying Dan. The parting of
their ways came when Johnny joined the Mohawk Minstrels, with
whom he remained nearly twenty years. Yet Drury Lane played its
part in his career, for he appeared there, notably as Grist in "The
Babes In The Wood" of 1907, and Alderman Fitzwarren in the
"Dick Whittington" of 1908, in several pantomimes. The range
of his stage experience was broadened by musical comedy, comic
opera and drama.

According to Mr. Shaw Desmond's *London Nights of Long Ago*,
Johnny always began his songs by grinning broadly and running the
tips of his fingers, after licking them, over his hair. Despite his
"om-bong-pong" he was the lightest man on his feet of that day,
save Dan Leno:

Nobody could hit a tambourine like Johnny. I have seen him hit it and
make sweet music out of it with nose, eyes, head, feet, elbows—everything but his hand . . . and how he could run it trilling down his leg!

*   *   *   *   *

There must be no confusing Johnny Danvers with Billy Danvers,
who was at Drury Lane the Christmas Eve of 1934. Where he is
it is always pantomime. In a green-baize apron, he is plainly the
gardener who lets the grounds of the Sleeping Beauty's castle get in
such a bad state. In Eton suit and topper, he is Buttons in costume
for the grand finale. There is a Christmas ring about his reason for
refusing to go into a nursing-home—the doctors might send him back,
as they did Aunt Ellen, with a baby. And his ideas about love have
obviously been gained through living in the house of Widow
Twankey. "It is nothing," he assured us, "for a man in love to put
the candle in bed and blow himself out." These philosophisings
may have been left out when Charles Perrault set fairy tales down in
writing, but directly we bring Cinderella, Red Riding Hood and
Blue Beard to life upon the stage, our instincts teach us that one of
their authentic companions must ever have been Billy Danvers.

As the Sleeping Beauty of two Drury Lane pantomimes, the
Princess of "Puss In Boots" and "Puss In New Boots," Joy in "Babes
In The Wood," and lastly Cinderella, Florence Smithson took with
her the glamour of "once upon a time" on her variety tours round
the world. She had a doll-like face and figure, and her top notes
and trills seemed to come from some pretty singing toy. At her
death in 1936, it was strange to realise that in two or three years she
would have been celebrating the golden jubilee of her career. She
was born at Leicester in 1884, and her father, a provincial manager,
put her in pantomime at the age of three. When she was playing
in "The Arcadians" in town her happiness seemed assured. But

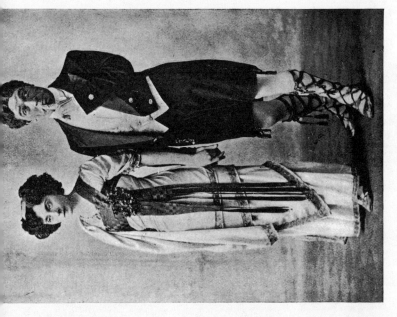

43   FLORENCE SMITHSON AND DAN ROLYAT
IN "THE ARCADIANS"

42   QUEENIE LEIGHTON, PRINCIPAL BOY OF
FOUR DRURY LANE PANTOMIMES

44 A PORTRAIT OF HARRY FRAGSON, A VERY GOOD LIKENESS, ON A
FRENCH SONG-FRONT

at Newcastle during the tour that followed, Dan Rolyat slipped
from the horse he rode as Simplicitas and severely injured his back.

PRINCE'S THEATRE, BRISTOL,
Return to ROYAL, Holborn, and SOUTH LONDON PALACE—EASTER.

THE GRIFFITHS BROTHERS

Through an illness which seemed at first to be incurable, she nursed
him devotedly. Afterwards they separated, and both remarried.

I

She never forgot him. He returned to the stage and was successful
for a time, before he was doomed to a lingering death from disease
in his tongue, and then she helped to raise subscriptions for him until
his death in 1927. Outwardly she always seemed a doll.

And last the pantomime horse—who is also the music-hall horse.
Just as we believe that Hamlet's existence is independent of the flesh
and blood of the actor who plays him, so we know Pogo of the
Griffiths Brothers as if he were our dearest dumb friend. He is an
immortal, no more meant for death than "The Bronze Horse" whose
tune he gallops to. Griffiths may come and Griffiths may go, but he
goes on for ever.

To remember the original "Brothers" of this name is to confess
to middle-age, for Joe Griffiths, who gave them their name, died
(at the age of forty-nine) in 1901. Can you recall their Blondin
Donkey or their wrestling lion, or their strong man burlesque, or
their famous pantomime animals of Drury Lane forty years ago?
All these monsters were in part "possessed of" Fred Delaney (otherwise Fred Griffith)—if I may be so uncivil as to speak of him as though
he were a devil inside them. After a farewell performance in the
spring of 1927, he yielded up the front legs to young Delaney, who
handed over the hindquarters to Harry Tate, junior.

Pogo himself does not change no matter what goes on inside
his hide. He still defies humanity. That he is stupid you can see
directly his head peers, cocked on one side, round the wings; that
he is peevish and malicious becomes plain when he sulks, and when he
sits down to shake with laughter at the discomfiture of Miss Lutie,
his trainer. Pogo is more than human. By the attitude he strikes,
you may recognise moods of cowardice, vanity, perversity and
self-importance that make Falstaffian creatures lovable. His self-
importance is certainly justified. Did he not eclipse all the modern
witticisms of Noel Coward when put through his paces by Miss
Lutie in a smart Cochran revue? In "Jack And The Beanstalk," the
Drury Lane 1935-6 pantomime, Pogo became a cow. When sold
for the bag of gold that turned into a bag of beans, he or she expressed
regret with a sentimentality that had been singularly absent from his
character as a horse. But whenever the Griffiths Brothers inside the
cowhide had to show off his and her paces the old spirit was as
rampant as ever.

45 THE OLD VIC., AS "THE ROYAL VICTORIA COFFEE PALACE AND MUSIC HALL"

From "The Graphic" of August 20, 1881

46, 47 ALBERT CHEVALIER

From photographs by his brother

CHAPTER SIX

Costers and Cockneys

UNLIKE the Cockney as popularly defined, the coster of our day was not born within the sound of Bow Bells. Yet he was a true Londoner. After Sam Weller's time, when Bartholomew Fair was no longer proclaimed in Smithfield, there was a great migration to Camberwell of the City's people from their haunts between Cheapside and Leather Lane. Long before Falstaff abused "these costermonger times," Cockneys had sold "costard apples"; and when they settled down round about the Old Kent Road, those who prospered well enough to buy "mokes and barrers" became a separate race from those, strong men mostly, who by digging inland navigation canals became known as "navvies." The costers' lovingly-groomed donkeys with barrows, and ponies in the shafts of daintily painted carts, you can still see in Regent's Park when prize-giving day comes round. These are often driven by "pearlies" with hospital collecting boxes, who are products of self-conscious pride in wearing clothes covered in pearl buttons (such as the vanishing race of costers never wore in such profusion), and dislike to be called costers.

Down in "Camberwell, sarf-east" these Londoners of the genuine old stock spoke a language [1] of their own, wore their own costume, and held their festivals—Derby Day on Epsom Downs, Easter Monday on Hampstead Heath, August Bank Holiday on the Welsh Harp (a sheet of water that once had that shape before corners were reclaimed for building sites), which was Hendon way, and every summer Saturday night on Peckham Rye. Winter sent them into taprooms, where Cockney kindliness and Irish devilment broke into song. Strange how our sense of humour has since removed itself from London to Lancashire and Yorkshire, and from Ireland to Scotland. Let me remind you that Lauder began by singing Irish songs and Wilkie Bard by singing Cockney songs—each of them while still in his native North—before I come back to Cockaigne.

As a latter-day Cockney, the coster sprang upon "the boards" through the same impulse that brought the Scot. Both appeared when the taproom atmosphere of the old halls cleared away, and

[1] The idea that it began with the Wellers is nonsense. Jerry Sneak in Foote's comedy, "The Mayor Of Garratt" (1763) says he " vill wisit my friends at Vitsontide."

audiences were prepared for a change from alcoholic humour with its stress on the mirth to be found in the misfortunes of wretched old women. The new fashion in songs and singers began in the 'nineties. Though mothers-in-law, lodgers, chuckers-out, and booze were still themes that knocked at the heart when Marie Lloyd and Dan Leno sang of them, newcomers had to find fresh topics. Victorian propriety was passing and people no longer wanted to wallow as a relief from the strain of living up to it. There were saner, sweeter notes in the new songs.

They came in with Albert Chevalier, the coster's laureate. "I was born," he wrote, "in London at 21 St. Ann's Villas, Royal Crescent, Notting Hill, on the 21st March 1861." As a child he recited at local Penny Readings, and became an actor in 1877 under the Bancrofts. While on the legitimate stage he wrote "Our 'Armonic Club" for himself in burlesque at the Strand, and "'Ave A Glass Along O' Me" for Lonnen at the Gaiety. The former of these was taken to the halls by Charles Coburn, who persuaded the author and composer to take his next songs there himself. Chevalier had fearful misgivings. The first offer, from the Alhambra, he refused. The second, from the London Pavilion, he accepted. A night or two beforehand, he stood at the back of the circle there while Bessie Bellwood was on the stage :

The boys in the gallery started chaffing, or, as she would have called it, "chipping" her, but they didn't stand the ghost of a chance. The wittiest "god" that ever hurled satire at a stage favourite, from the security of Olympian heights, would only attempt it with Bessie, knowing full well that he would come off second best. I had often witnessed her performance, but now it had a special or personal interest for me. I was to appear before those very "chippies." Where should I be if they started chaffing during my performance, as they were at the moment with Miss Bellwood ?

He said to the manager, "You've made a big mistake." But at his début on the night of February 2, 1891, there was no doubt of his success with one of the quietest, most sensitive, songs he ever sang :

> You ain't forgotten how we drove that day
> Dahn to the Welsh 'Arp, in my donkey shay ?
> Folks with a "chy-ike" shouted, "Ain't they smart ?"
> You looked a queen, me every inch a Bart.
> Seemed that the moke was saying, "Do me proud,
> Mine is the nobbiest turn-out in the crowd."
> Me in my "pearlies" felt a toff that day,
> Dahn at the Welsh 'Arp which is 'Endon way.

He showed a delighted audience what the aborigine of London was really like. There were resemblances to Jenny Hill's 'Arry and to Vance's Chickaleery Bloke, but Albert Chevalier had studied his subject in the streets, not halls. He had watched 'Enery 'Awkins walking out with 'Liza and dancing with her that Cockney holiday dance which is far more exhilarating than all the Morris dances, country dances, and nigger dances in the world. It all came so naturally to Chevalier that he thought little of his title, "The Coster's Laureate," and more of his early ambition to be an actor. So the singer of such masterpieces as "Knocked 'Em In The Old Kent Road" and "The Future Mrs. 'Awkins," would make embarrassed feelings run up and down our spines with a musical monologue, called "The Old Bachelor" that ended:

> They call me woman hater!—if they only knew the truth!
> That somewhere, where the flowers are seen,
> A white cross marks the spot I mean,
> Who keeps a little grave so green?
> A poor old bachelor.

Audiences applauded him in this vein, and all his many imitators in concert parties preferred it, because in it they could emulate him, while in his coster studies they could not. Consequently the mistake had no ill results for him until his last appearances in variety shortly before his death in the summer of 1923. A public that contained few of his old admirers might listen with respect to famous coster songs they had heard in the nursery. But when this old star asked them to look on him, in a solemn recitation, as Napoleon, there was almost an end to his welcome.

* * * * *

Some fuss was excited when a gramophone record made by Tennyson, talked under the needle. There is always a thrill in becoming vividly linked with the past. And if sounds from a wax disc or the sight of an old tin photograph can do this, how much greater is the stir when a living person walks straight from the past into the present? This is what happened when Gus Elen came back a few years ago. Veterans who never leave us, change with the changing years; others who retire for a time, return a little older and more old-fashioned— they do not arouse in us our peculiar emotions on beholding the golden dustman, the postman on holiday, and the caustic Covent Garden porter, once again. These are not merely recollections of the past. They are the past.

When they were invented, such types did walk London streets, although now you may only see them in old lithographs and woodcuts. Yet on the boards Gus Elen treads, you behold no careful reconstructions by an antiquarian, but the reflection of the life around

him by a comedian. That life has vanished : he remains. To see him
at the footlights once again is like meeting a familiar figure in the yard
of a coaching inn and realising that his name is Sam Weller. There
is certainly closer relationship between the Cockney characters of
Dickens's London and Gus Elen than between him and those who
dwell within sound of Bow Bells now. Compared with Gus Elen,
Little Tich was modern and George Robey futurist.

Those who cannot be amazed by Gus Elen have no ears to hear or
eyes to see. Directly he swung jauntily into view at the Palladium
the Cockney of a bygone day came back to life. This is genuine
character. The way he walks and twists his features, the cut of his
corduroy clothes, and the angle at which he wears his flapped cap are
expressive, not of a determination to be funny at all costs, but of
fidelity to the Cockney who once belonged to real life. Young people
who talk of "a nice quiet day" without knowing where the words
come from, hail the Victorian postman with delight. Similarly, with
"'E Dunno Where 'E Are" : it is permanently part of our speech.
"Down The Road," "Never Introduce Yer Donah To A Pal," "If It
Wasn't For The 'Ouses In Between," "Yer Could Almost Shut Yer
Eyes And 'Ear Them Grow," "Wait Till The Work Comes Round,"
and "The Cove Wot's Lived In London All 'Is Life," are no older
than the 'nineties. In inspiration they go back to the 'seventies, when
young Elen was practising how to black up in order to sing at
"pubs." Here is one sound argument for not moving with the
times : if he had, he could not move us so deeply at the thought of
what time has destroyed—a place that was not a collection of cos-
mopolitan influences, but London town.

★   ★   ★   ★   ★

Amid the Palladium's large assembly of old stars for the finale of
the Royal Variety Performance of 1935, none was more brightly
arrayed than Kate Carney. In a towering hat of coloured ostrich
feathers and a gown of red, white, and blue, picked out in shiny little
buttons, she looked like the empress of all the "pearlies." When she
sang two of her old coster ditties, the whole audience took up the
refrain under the eyes of King George V and Queen Mary. Behind
her, older performers (notably Alice Leamer) from their home at
Brinsworth, "dudes," "heavy swells," heroes of the battlefield,
Hebrew comedians, nigger minstrels, and one veteran of the hand-
bells, began to prance and wave their arms in time to her tunes.

If you have ever had a liking for the life of London streets, Kate
Carney will appeal to you as Burns does to a Scotsman. In herself
she may not hold a candle to Dan Leno, Marie Lloyd, or Little Tich,
but her songs are the best the Cockney has ever added to the verses

48, 49 GUS ELEN. FROM A SONG-FRONT AND A PHOTOGRAPH

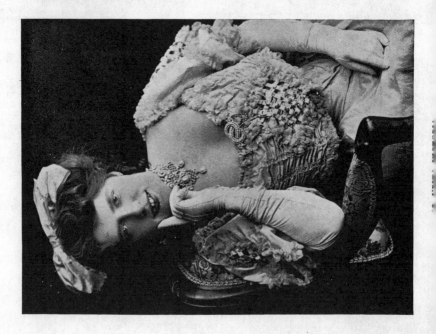

of our land. Set them side by side with the lyrics of that country bumpkin, William Shakespeare. While he boasts of merrily henting stiles, Kate describes what it feels like to play "tanner marf organs" round the houses. While he praises lambkins, she replies with "pen'norths of each" round at the fish-shop. While he invites "Then come kiss me sweet and twenty," she speaks of love with "No blokes shall come and kiss yer or for them I shall go." And in one respect she has a decided advantage. Her "What ho" is more alive than his "Hey nonino."

As the daughter of one of the Brothers Raynard, well known on the halls seventy or eighty years ago, she made her first public appearance on February 10, 1890, at the Albert—a peculiar building, since it was actually the Imperial Theatre removed stone by stone from Westminster and rebuilt stone by stone at Canning Town. Here she started as the singer of an Irish song until her true destiny overcame her. She remained a public idol for many years, and appeared at the Royal Variety Performance at the Palace in 1912. After the War she retired for a brief spell and came back to challenge the craze for American syncopation, by showing the younger generation what the old halls could do. Yet she compromised with the new spirit. The setting for her turn was a frame of draped curtains instead of the old-fashioned street corner "drop," and she wore a "latest creation" from Paris instead of the old frills and furbelows.

But she would not stomach any collection of "hot" players with saxophones; no, since she had to have a band on the stage, it must be true Cockney tradition, and we were treated to a procession of mouth-organists. Once more we heard the tunes which warmed us in our early youth. Hardly one was missing, for she gave us simply the chorus of each, so that there should be no disappointment. Each time she quoted the refrain of some popular syncopated song before capping it with one of her incomparable ditties of London life—"Has Anyone Seen My Yiddisher Boy?" "Three Pots A Shilling," "Got Any Letters For Me," and best of all, "Liza Johnson."

She retired again, and came back again in style. She stood on the stage in a scene of "a beautiful mansion surrounded by riches untold," a butler who "accompanied her on the piano," and a housemaid who joined in the choruses. As she changed the song, the window curtains parted to disclose tableaux in illustration of the verses. The postman brought letters, the errand-boy loved his mother, the hot-potato can glowed in the shadow of Big Ben, and the donkey drew his barrow-load of three pots a shilling. After introducing us to "My daughter, Dorothy, and my grand-daughter, Gana," Kate added, "Not so bad for seventy-two." That was in 1932. But when she celebrated her golden wedding just before the Royal Variety Performance in 1935, she mentioned that when she was married to George Barclay, the Cockney step-dancer, in 1885, her age was sixteen.

★　★　★　★　★

Exactly when Harry Champion was born no one knows besides himself, and he won't say. Nor is the date of his first public appearance on record, but it must have been a long time ago. All that we can discover is that he was originally a negro comedian who was billed as "Will Conray" at the Queen's, Poplar—which is still on the active list—and the Parthenon, Greenwich, on February 27, 1888. For years he could have announced his jubilee any day he wanted to. What he did announce instead, very dramatically, was his farewell performance. A few minutes later he was surprised to be asked about it. He goes on singing "The End Of Me Old Cigar," "Ginger, You're Barmy," "'Enery The Eighth," and his other classics, in the rapid manner he made famous all those years ago.

Like other idols of the halls, he was in danger from "the disease of personal popularity." The cure he tried was job-mastering. That was why he took to the business of driving people to and from race-meetings, which still occupies all his spare time at Wood Green. His stage name is not over the business, but he is hard at work there all the same.

"No," he says, "I have not made a fortune out of it. That story got about in the old days when I used to let broughams out on hire to my brother 'pros.' I never went into the business for profit. I started it because I like to see a bit of the country myself, and I went on with it to keep off the drink. It was necessary. As soon as a man made his name on the halls in the old days, everybody wanted to stand him a tiddly. That's just what I wanted to keep clear of. One day I was polishing my own cab windows—half-crown a day job— when a lady and gentleman stopped by my side. 'Huh,' said I to the glass as I breathed on it.

'Aren't you the Mr. Champion who made us laugh so much last night?' said the gentleman.

'Huh,' I said to the glass as I nodded.

'I'm sorry you've had to come to this,' said the gentleman, 'won't you share a bottle of wine with us?'

'Gotter to clean this winder,' said I as though my life depended on it, and he went away feeling very sorry for me. But I had to save my life, hadn't I?"

When asked why he made no use of his stage name in the business, he answered, "It's not my real name and never was. Somebody gave it to me. It was all through a dislike the manager of the Marylebone took to me after I had been there for nine months at the time I was

52 HARRY CHAMPION

From a photograph by Joan England

53 THE EMPIRE BY NIGHT IN 1895

From a photograph by Paul Martin

known as Will Conray. I went on tour for a bit. When I came back, he told my agent he'd have nothing to do with me. 'Right,' said the agent, 'but you might give a new man his chance.' 'Who is he?' asked the manager, and then and there my agent baptized me 'Harry Champion' and came and told me afterwards. They didn't know me that night, because I had a batch of new songs and blacked up for only one of them. But after 'God Save the King' they saw the name of 'Will Conray' on my band parts. There *was* a row. But the manager himself said I'd 'paralysed 'em,' and so I stayed for another nine months.

"In those days I was singing 'When The Old Dun Cow Caught Fire.' Outside the Bull Inn at Chatham one night, Lord Savernake, who had taken me in to have one, said he could sing it better than I could. He was a rum 'un if you like. Everybody called him 'Ducks.' 'Born outside my own class,' he used to say of himself, and he drove a coster's cart, wearing 'pearlies'—in Rotten Row. He married out of the chorus—a nice girl she was too.

"Well, that night I'm speaking of, the policeman didn't want him to sing and asked him not to. All he did was to tell that policeman to referee, before taking hold of him by the buttons, and starting my song all over again. The next morning Lord Savernake was fined ten shillings.

"I thought of 'What Cheer Me Old Brown Son, 'Ow Are Yer,' at my father's funeral. He was a very jolly man, and that was a saying of his whenever he met anybody. His friends had sent a floral harp with 'To The Old Brown Son' on it. On the way back, I said to my sister, 'I think he'd like me to make a song out of that.' When I got home I wrote it down at once, and so his saying spread all over England.

"I suppose you know I started all this jazz stuff. Music-hall performances used to last from six to half-past twelve then, with long waits between the turns so that the waiters could fetch drinks and the chairman could be offered one. My wife used to go to the stage hands as soon as I was ready and tell them to ring up. If they refused, she said, 'Very well, I'll pull the curtain up myself.' Then I began at once in the quick-firing-gun style I invented, and I finished three songs and a dance before the manager had come back from seeing a man about a dog.

"I did a hornpipe. You had to dance in those days or run the risk of losing your life. The only way to escape if you weren't a dancer was to wear jinks on your heels—you know, those bits of metal that go clickety-click. I did that. It makes everybody say 'Fine dancer' before you start. Anyhow, I had a name when I was eighteen."

There was a time—some years ago now—when Harry Champion

told an audience, "I don't often work now—I can't get it." They applauded him so warmly that tears came into his eyes. "Don't cry, Harry," came a voice from the gallery, full of brotherly tenderness. He pulled himself together, and as the "tabs" closed in front of him we heard his feet perform the double-shuffle while his voice was heard singing, "Any Old Iron." At a concert given to disabled soldiers by Joe Elvin at a garden-party, these two sang "Jolly Old Pals." On that ballad the sun never sets, but it is doubtful whether there ever was a time when it was so *historically* sung.

The most triumphant moment of Harry Champion's life occurred in a Palladium scene which represented the old Empire promenade. After all the younger stars had given imitations of older stars, he came on and gave the audience the real thing. How everybody, on the stage as well as off, cheered.

THE COSTER'S SING-SONG IN "THE NAG'S HEAD" AT THE CLERKENWELL END
OF LEATHER LANE

From "Paul Pry," Dec. 13, 1856

SUNG BY MACKNEY THE INIMITABLE

POLLY CROW

WRITTEN & COMPOSED EXPRESSLY FOR HIM BY

G. W. HUNT

COMPOSER OF THE 'ORGAN GRINDER' 'SUGAR SHOP' &c

ENT. STA HALL

PRICE 3/-

LONDON. J CAMPBELL &c 11, ARGYLE PLACE, REGENT STREET. W.

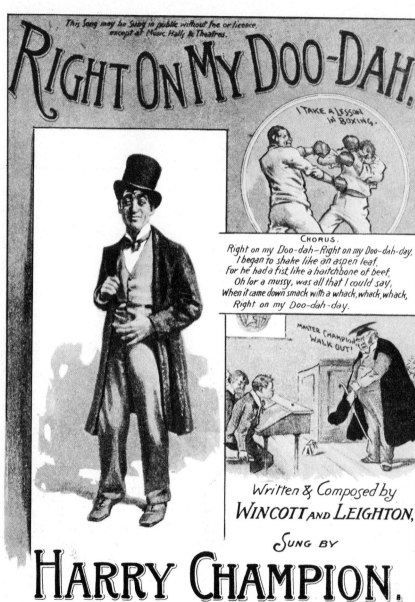

54   ONE OF HARRY CHAMPION'S EARLIER SUCCESSES

(On Reverse)   55   MACKNEY AGAINST A LONDON "DROP"

CHAPTER SEVEN

Nigger Minstrels

BURNT cork, we used to think, could be seen but not heard. If that were the whole truth we should not have witnessed so many recent revivals of interest in it, for the modern vogues have been mainly due to records and broadcasting. We were asking one another, "Er, what causes dat?" and "Er, who cares 'bout dat?" long before the Two Black Crows appeared on the screen. We were taught these words when we listened to the gramophone. By wireless we had a close acquaintance with Alexander and Mose long before they showed themselves "in the flesh," and then the rush to see them was not because their humour needed any help from sight.

All this goes to prove that nigger minstrel humour is no mere matter of "blacking up." Yet it used to be nothing more than that, and still is with performers far more notable than the second cousins many times removed of Uncle Bones, who sing the songs of Araby with one foot and a nose inside the saloon-bar door—very reasonably ignoring the notice, "No musicians." At a time no more remote than their youth, nigger minstrelsy was a large, happy, placid reservoir. It ran into the broad stream of the music-hall and was drained dry.

Listen and you may imagine the music of that cascade yet. Mackney may be before your time, although the title of his song, "The Whole Hog Or None" is frequently mentioned, while the Ethiopian Serenaders of Evans's Song and Supper Rooms have long vanished without leaving any such relic behind. To the new generation even Eugene Stratton and Chirgwin are also only a legend and a name, and even "Black Justice," acted by Big Ben Brown, Newland and Leclerc, is forgotten apart from echoes of its great joke :

MAGISTRATE: Are yo' guilty or not guilty?
PRISONER: Not guilty, jedge.
MAGISTRATE: Then what the Dickens yo' doin' here—wastin' our time?

But the songs that were originally orchestrated for the bones, the banjo, and the tambourine are with us still, and scores of others that we think of as typical of the British music-hall were composed by the melodists—some (Americans) unknown here—of burnt cork.

Among them was Henry Sayers. You may remember reading about

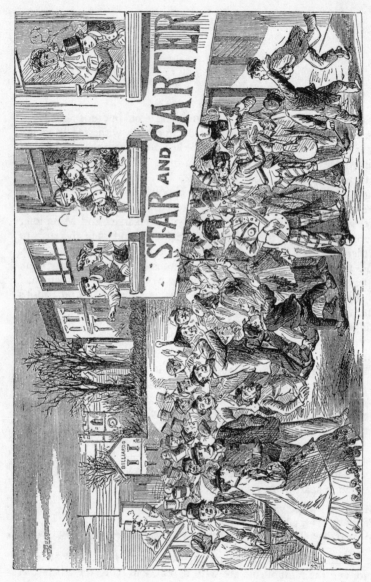

WANDERING MINSTRELS AT RICHMOND
From Tallis' "Illustrated Life in London," April 2, 1864

57 THE MOHAWK'S INTERLOCUTOR
From coloured song-fronts

56 WHEN CHIRGWIN WAS SLIM

58 MACKNEY'S DISPLAY-BOARD

his death at the age of seventy-seven in 1934. *The Times* recalled how he had once been the manager of a minstrel troupe. While walking through the coloured quarter of St. Louis he heard a tumult of voices rising out of a dive. Down below he found a negress singing an unending song, unfit for squeamish ears, with the refrain of "Tin-a-ling-a-ling-a-boomderay." The chorus had such an intoxicating effect that Sayers fitted it fresh verses and tried it in his show. Possibly it was first played by minstrels as soon as they detrained and went marching down Main Street, calling back "How-dees" in answer to shouts from old cronies, with a drum-major at the head of their parade.

Certainly "Ta-Ra-Ra-Boom-De-Ay" was included in the score of "Tuxedo"—a title derived from the club in Tuxedo Park, New York, which caused the dinner jacket to be called a "Tuxedo" in America —when Thatcher's Minstrels tried to revolutionise the entertainment by giving it the form of musical comedy; yet Sayer's song was by

LOTTIE COLLINS
From "Footlights," Judy's Annual for 1895

no means the hit of the show, which became popular because of half a dozen other numbers, notably "Sweet Marie"—written by one of the company. "Ta-Ra-Ra-Boom-De-Ay" had to be plugged in London first before it could create such a rage in America that Lottie Collins obtained £200 a week while singing it from the Atlantic Coast to the Pacific. Whenever the dance-bands play it now our inward eye sees a vision of her wasp waist, flying curls and high-kicking high-heeled shoes amid a froth of lace. In "Tuxedo" it began :

> A sweet Tuxedo girl you see,
> Queen of swell so-ci-e-ty.

When it was brought to London in 1891, an English version—
there were others later—was written under the original title by
B. M. Batchelor, whose first verse began :

> Once a young man went to woo,
> Just as foolish chaps will do.
> In the garden sat with Sue,
> And exchanged a kiss or two.

That was "sensationally popularised" by Lottie Collins in "Dick
Whittington" at the Grand, Islington, in 1891. Harry Randall,
who played Idle Jack, declared that her "abandon dance" was encored
until she became exhausted. Once or twice she fainted in the wings.

Meanwhile George Edwardes needed a fresh attraction for his
burlesque, "Cinder-Ellen Up Too Late," at the Gaiety. His first
misfortune was that Nellie Farren had been too ill to play the name
part. His second set-back was the national mourning for the Duke
of Clarence. It was customary then to introduce music-hall songs
into burlesque, but not with their original singers. Edwardes
realised that this time no substitute would do. Consequently Lottie
Collins had to be persuaded to rush from Islington and back nightly
in order to join the wedding party in the Palace scene of the Gaiety
burlesque. She began in a trembling voice while gently waving her
handkerchief. Suddenly, putting her hands on her tightly corsetted
waist to the signal of a bang on the drum, she changed into a bacch-
analian fury, growing "half-maddened" as the orchestra played the
refrain more and more wildly. The audience shouted with a delight
which spread all through the town. National mourning was forgotten. The Gaiety was besieged.

Then the parodies began. Harry Randall's at Islington was
followed by Tom Costello's "All-Through Ta-Ra-Ra-Boom-De-
Ay," and Katie Lawrence's "Oh! Ta-Ra-Ra." Then there were
imitations such as "Br-Room-De-Doo-Dum!" They are all—over
a score—forgotten, but the original is played to this day.

Several other songs that have made music-hall history came from
Nigger Minstrelsy. "Bill Bailey" was composed by a member of
an American troupe. "Pony" Moore wrote the music of "Blind
Boy," and Harry Hunter, the Mohawks' interlocutor, the words of
"My Fiddle Is My Sweetheart," the most popular songs of Chirgwin,
the "White-Eyed Kaffir." No song was ever demanded more
insistently than "Blind Boy." There was a night at the London
Pavilion when Chirgwin—his Christian name of George was rarely
mentioned—asked the "Ladies and Gen'plum" if he could be excused.
"Blind Boy," shouted the gallery. Chirgwin came back to explain
that he was due at "The Temple" (the Temple of Varieties, Hammer-

smith). "Blind Boy," shouted the gallery. "If you can't be quiet I'll
have you all turned out," said the manager. "Blind Boy," shouted
the gallery. They were all, still shouting for it, turned out.

Year after year he had to sing it whether he wanted to or no.
"Blind Boy? Yes, I was last night!" he often replied in his thin,
piping voice. How the widely-credited story got about that the
song was inspired by the blindness of a son of his own, he never
knew. Probably there was no more truth in the legend that his
lozenge-shaped "white-eye" first took shape through his rubbing
the burnt cork away where a fly, one hot night, was trying to settle.
He was billed as "The White-Eyed Kaffir," in 1877, and before that
he was "The White-Eyed Musical Moke," which takes us back to
the days when he was one of the Brothers Chirgwin. He began as
one of the Chirgwin family at the Swallow Rooms, Piccadilly, in 1861.

In the 'eighties he played kings in Sara Lane's pantomimes at the
"Old Brit," Hoxton. "King Trickee; or, Harlequin, The Beetle,
The Sporting Duchess And The Golden Casket" was one, and "King
Kookoo; or, Harlequin Bon-Bon And The Golden Serpent" another.
His jubilee was celebrated at the Oxford in 1911. The next year he
appeared at the Palace in the first Royal Variety Performance. Only
Marie Lloyd was better loved by the public than he. He died in
1922 at the age of sixty-seven.

In his early days, when he was "thin enough to go through a
barrel," Chirgwin played the banjo. When he grew so corpulent
that the black jersey he wore began to stretch, he played the 'cello.
But his favourite instrument was the one-stringed fiddle. He would
play the violin, too, and other musical instruments we never saw in
his hands. Both he and his songs are ranked among "comics," but
the two by which he is remembered were not to make us laugh.

They are relics of the good old days of Nigger Minstrelsy. There
was a great difference between the music-hall and minstrelsy, no
matter how many songs and singers passed from one to the other.
While the one thrived on its bad reputation, the other died because
it catered principally for Victorian family parties. Minstrelsy was
steadfastly sabbatarian. Even though the licensing experts of the
London County Council still, to this very day, ban the daubing of
burnt cork on the face of any singer in a Sunday concert, they would
find nothing for censure in the programmes of the St. James's Hall
and the Agricultural Hall at a time when Christmas pantomimes
were constantly wounding the feelings of the righteous.

Imagine the feelings of children who were taken to see McNish,
Johnson and Slavin's Refined Minstrels, and what they must have
thought of an "ideal programme" which contained one mildly comic
song among a dozen such as "Mother's Last Good-bye," "Angel

Voices In My Dreams," and "Creep Into Bed, My Baby, Or One
Little Kiss For Mama," to offset the knockabout sketches. The morbid
and lugubrious became the minstrels' stand-by in the days when their
chief care was to let wealthy maiden aunts enjoy a good cry over
"Close The Shutters, Willie's Dead," "Keep Pretty Flowers On My
Grave," "Place A Headstone Over My Grave," "Driven From Home,"
and "Kiss Me, Mother, Ere I Die." Next, water was used for mixing
instead of beer when the singers blacked up—though they were so
insistent on burning nothing but champagne corks that the same
breath that blew down St. James's Hall has been blamed for the fall
in champagne imports.

Their history is told in *Minstrel Memories* by Harry Reynolds.
On first looking into it you may fancy that the wrong illustrations
have been bound up with the book. Who are these dignified Victorians, formed into imposing groups? Surely a mere smearing of
burnt cork would not have transformed them into interlocutors and
corner-men? Yet they were not more respectable in their private
appearance than in their public entertainments. The Mohawks
announced "Operatic Nights" and "Classical Nights." They also
had military nights when "Just Before The Battle, Mother," was in
great demand, and nautical nights with "The Death Of Nelson."
From their sacred concerts "enough people were turned away to fill
the big hall twice over." No doubt the minstrels were very warmly
admired by grown-ups at this time, but boys brought up on "Tears
Are Blessings, Let Them Flow," and "Do Not Nurse Your Anger"
—the Mohawks were famous for such wholesome sentiments—became
men who caused the music-hall boom in the hey-day of Bessie Bellwood and Marie Lloyd.

There is no need to delve into a very remote past. The real boom
began in the early 'forties. Edwin P. Christy, a melancholy American
who committed suicide in 1862 because he was afraid of losing his
savings through the Civil War, never came to England, but ex-
members of his troupe made his name famous over here when they
opened at the smaller St. James's Hall, Piccadilly, on April 11, 1859.
On settling down they sent offers to leading American minstrels to
join them. The news reached George Washington Moore, who
sailed without an invitation. What manner of man he was, Mr.
Reynolds describes:

The youngest of a family of thirteen he was born on the anniversary of
George Washington's birthday, so his parents thought fit to christen him
George Washington Moore, although, as Moore said, "Whereas George
Washington refused to tell a lie, I've been telling lies for a living all my life."
When he was eight, his father died, so he had to try and earn his own living
at a very early age.

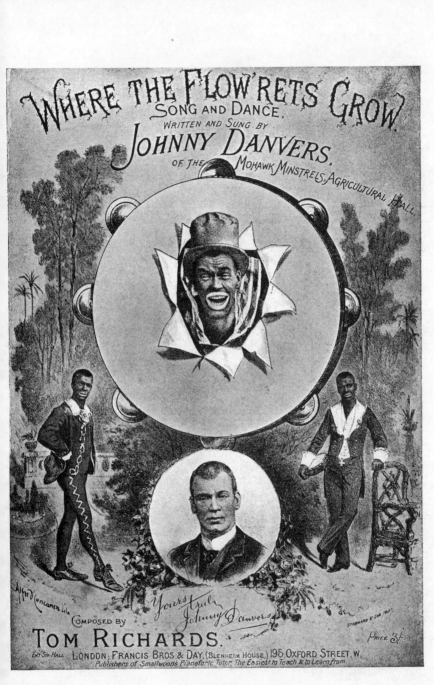

59 A JOHNNY DANVERS SONG—FRONT

61 FREDERICK BURGESS WITH THE CALCULATING EYE

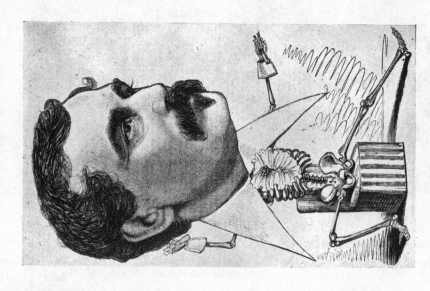

60 "PONY" MOORE WITH THE BONES

While still a boy he learnt to drive forty ponies at a time in Franconi's Circus, New York, and this, according to our author, was why he was christened "Pony" Moore. The other explanation is that when he backed a horse it was always for a "pony" (£25). He claimed to have been the first minstrel to play the bones.

The director of the Christy Minstrels in London disbanded the troupe and returned to America. Four years later Moore formed a troupe of his own, engaged Frederick Burgess to be his acting-manager at thirty shillings a week, made the St. James's Hall his headquarters, and flourished. One day each year he took his benefit at two performances. After the second, Mrs. Pony Moore, wearing diamonds worth a king's ransom, would "receive." Then came a ball and a supper, as Emily Soldene tells:

Such a supper! and such a company! all the prettiest women in London, and all the best men. Dukes, earls, marquises and lords intrigued for invites. About 4.30 a.m., Pony, mounting the table, would make a speech welcoming his guests, and finish up by telling them he was a free-born American, and what he had paid for the champagne.

In time Moore and Burgess began to quarrel. During a particularly heated outburst, Moore told Burgess to go. According to Mr. Reynolds, Burgess did go; but he went no farther than the office of the ground-landlord and offered himself as a new tenant of the St. James's Hall. As he secured a long lease in his own name, the foes became partners until Burgess died at Burgess Hall, Finchley, in 1893. Moore, who retired the next year, died in 1909, nearly ninety years of age, at Moore Lodge, Finchley Road. The Moore and Burgess Minstrels gave their last performance at the St. Leonard's Pier Pavilion in 1900.

Nobody else has described St. James's Hall so vividly as Shaw Desmond. This, from *London Nights of Long Ago*, conjures up its atmosphere:

What a bare hall it was! The forms on the floor with high, hard backs, the flinty gallery; the shallow stage with the "niggers" in layers each above the other; the half score of musicians, and, the only touch of colour, the two lines of reserved seats with red upholstery for the infrequent swell.

Harry Hunter was a magnificent interlocutor of about six feet three. In his white kid gloves and spotless shirt-front he "sat like a Life Guardsman on his horse" as he solemnly addressed the end man:

"Good evening, Joe."

"Good evening, Mr. Hunter."

"I have heard that you were seen last night walking down the Strand in company with a nice young lady."

"You heard that I was seen last night walking down the Strand with a

nice young lady, Mr. Hunter?" the end man would ask, for all questions
were repeated, so as to give the not too quick audience a chance to hear
them—also it added to the effect and followed a certain prescribed ritual.

"Yes, I heard that you were seen going down the Strand . . ." Mr. Hunter
would reply.

The Mohawks were formed by James and William Francis, brothers
who were employed by a firm of music-publishers. When minstrelsy
needed all their attention in 1873, they took over the Berners Hall,
next to the Agricultural Hall, Islington, where they were joined by
Harry Hunter, who had been running another troupe and writing
songs and sketches. After some struggles they found larger quarters
in the St. Mary's Hall of the "Agricultural," and last of all moved,
when the Moore and Burgess Minstrels left London, to the St. James's
Hall in 1900, calling themselves the "Mohawk, Moore and Burgess
Minstrels" on the strength of having engaged two or three of their
old rivals. At the zenith of minstrelsy, Mr. Reynolds says, it almost
seemed that England was "divided into two classes—those who
wanted to become minstrels and those who did not." The former
became a nuisance that had to be stopped.

If a very bad case came along he was told, "You'll have to turn somer-
saults and do trapeze work if you come here. Don't worry, we'll teach you."
So the minstrels would strap a stout belt round his waist, hook the belt through
a rope that ran through a pulley overhead and haul him up nearly to the
ceiling, then after pelting him with cushions they would leave him suspended
while they went out to get a drink.

Once a large Irishman, who wanted to sing "The Death Of Nelson,"
was promised special "sound effects." Directly he appeared, dressed
as a sailor, the lights went out, discordant noises came from the
orchestra, and yells from the minstrels; pistol shots were fired on the
stage, and a bucket of water was thrown over him. A bird-mimic,
who used a hidden bird-warbler, was advised, "Go to Mr. Burgess
and tell him you want five pounds on account before you join the
troupe. If he objects don't be put off, but insist on it. Being a bit
of a joker he may pretend to be annoyed, but it will only be his fun."
When ordered out by Burgess he smiled (as directed), repeated his
demand for five pounds, and was kicked out. He was told to go back
and ask for ten pounds. Two minutes later he was seen "flying for
his life down Piccadilly."

Long after the St. James's Hall had been pulled down in 1904 to
make way for the Piccadilly Hotel, odd minstrels were still idolised
on the halls. Whenever Eugene Stratton sang Leslie Stuart's songs,
"Lily Of Laguna" more particularly, the old enthusiasm flared up
afresh. Leslie Stuart assured me that Laguna was a real place.

"If you are going from New Orleans to California," he explained solemnly, "it lies about a hundred miles on your left. Lily was a cave-dweller there. No, it is not on the map."

You need an atlas for this story all the same, for the composer was born at Southport three years after the singer of his song was born at Buffalo, near Niagara Falls, in 1861. Eugene Stratton's parents had come from Alsace. His mother died in Leslie Stuart's arms when he visited Buffalo.

Eugene Stratton first blacked up as a small boy in a saloon near his home. He came to London with Haverley's Minstrels, and stayed behind with Moore and Burgess at the St. James's Hall. He married one of Moore's daughters (and so became the brother-in-law of Fred Vokes, the pantomimist, and Charlie Mitchell, the heavyweight). There was little of the nigger minstrel or the real negro in the gentle coon he became when he sang Leslie Stuart's songs. He blurted out the words so wistfully and warbled the whistling solos so tenderly that he was sheer romance. In his soft shoes he danced as noiselessly on the darkened stage as a wraith. It was never a "set dance." He always improvised as he went along. He was an "idol of the halls" who never ceased to be worshipped until his death in 1918, at the age of fifty-seven.

Later still there was Frank Tinney, the black-faced bandmaster with bagpipes under his arm, who was one of the last variety stars at the old Empire. He did not sing—at least, he merely got to the end of the first line of his song before arguments with "Oinest," the conductor, started—but he did talk, on such subjects as "the gender of the canteloupe" and the best way to cook starlings, with bubbling humour.

CHAPTER EIGHT

Mashers

WHAT was known to one past generation as the "fop" and to another as the "dandy," became the "dude" and the "masher," the "swell" and the "toff." There was also the "chappie," who was of less social consequence, the "fellah" who had just turned sixteen, and the "Piccadilly Johnny With The Little Glass Eye." That indicates the range of Vesta Tilley's male impersonations. Among them are soldiers, sailors, militia-men, policeman and messenger-boy, as well as a curate or two, but even these belonged to that side of masculinity which is clothes conscious. All the young men she has pretended to be are proud of what they wear—all of them, from the one in "Etons" to the one in khaki.

For fifty years she paraded such types before our delighted eyes. There was more than imitation in her mannerisms. There was more than caricature. She was always a very ordinary youth, but she portrayed him in an extraordinary manner. We saw him not as we saw him in real life, or as he imagined himself, but as he appeared in the eyes of a clever, critically observant woman. Conjure up in your memory the portraits she painted of youth in the 'seventies, 'eighties, 'nineties, nineteen-hundreds, pre-war years and war years; in that picture gallery which now fills your mind there is the history of a period. And it is a history with a noteworthy moral.

Since there have been debates concerning how she began, we must refer to her own account of it in *Recollections of Vesta Tilley*. When she was three years of age—she was born on May 13, 1864, at Worcester—her father, Harry Ball, was chairman of a music-hall in Gloucester. On the night of his departure, he was given a complimentary benefit:

It was a red-letter night in my life, for my father decided that I should make my first public appearance on that occasion. It comes back to me as though it were yesterday. I remember the Hall filled with tobacco smoke and the fumes of beer, my father carrying me to the side of the stage, straightening my little skirts, the band striking up the music of my little medley, and his words of encouragement: "Don't be frightened. Sing as if you meant it. Don't cough, and speak clearly."

They moved to Nottingham, where he had been engaged as chair-

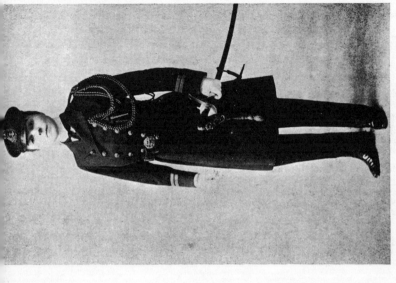

62, 63 VESTA TILLEY—FROM SONG-FRONT AND PHOTOGRAPH

man of the St. George's Hall, and there she was billed as "The Great Little Tilley." Not until she had "run through the whole gamut of female characters, from baby songs to old maids' ditties," was she caught posturing before the glass in her father's hat and coat—the well-known incident which gained for her the little evening suit, big enough for "an ordinary rabbit," that she treasures still. At the age of five she wore this and a large moustache in mimicry of Sims Reeves, at Birmingham. She also wore it on a return visit to Leicester, only to hear the chairman announce, "Ladies and gentlemen, I regret this interruption, but the band will play a selection while Little Tilley retires to take off her trousers and appear as we expect to see her." That set-back forgotten, she made such progress in her studies that on her arrival in London at the age of ten, audiences could not tell whether she was boy or girl. "Great Little" had to go. Three names, chosen from a list at the end of a dictionary, were written on slips of paper and put in her father's hat. The one she drew had written on it, "Vesta."

Truth to nature was so much her aim that her art might have been deemed contrary to the spirit of pantomime. Yet an engagement as Robinson Crusoe at Portsmouth, when she was thirteen, was only the first of many Boys, sometimes Second, but usually Principal. She prided herself on acting emotional scenes seriously and sincerely, but she entered into the spirit of topsy-turvydom all the same. There are photographs of her in all the feathers, fleshings, and feminine finery of Prince Charming, and there is a picture of her in doublet, hose—and bowler hat. She might have changed our idea of the Principal Boy if she had a mind to, but she was too good a trouper to upset its frolics. In all the scenes of the fairy tale she obeyed its rules and sang her own songs in between-whiles: "Quite A Toff In My Newmarket Coat," written and composed by her father, she sang in "Beauty And The Beast," at Birmingham in 1881. To compose songs for her was an honour many sought. Leslie Stuart provided her with "Sweetheart May," George Dance with "Angels Without Wings," and "Daughters," Walter de Freece with "A Simple Maiden," and Oswald Stoll with "Mary And John." Thus she numbered among those whom she inspired to write "words and music," three who were to be knighted.

Now is the time to describe the characters she created, for some of them are being forgotten. One such is "Burlington Bertie," with the Hyde Park drawl and the Bond Street crawl, whose memory has been obscured by Ella Shields' "Burlington Bertie From Bow"—a very different person. We must remember "Burlington Bertie" because he is the clue to Vesta Tilley's opinion of men. "He'll fight and he'll die like an Englishman," she sang in the midst of her mockery of his follies, which is a plain hint that Vesta Tilley's understanding sympathy for her "victims" has never been very far beneath the surface. That is precisely why we have always been hypnotised by them.

Go back to her portrait of one of the "rollicking, frolicking, devil-me-care young blades," who knocked down potmen and threw the village "slop" into the horse-pond. It is inspired by frank admiration of the young male, no matter how rowdy, which was probably her first feeling about him. You might also imagine she envied his zestful "nights out" on the spree; she even let him get tipsy with an air, whether or no that was true to life. But "A Nice Quiet Week," in which all these things happened, belonged to the days before she found herself.

Some of her songs in the 'eighties hardly bear the imprint of her personality at all. Some are of the kind any red-nosed comic or *serio comic* might have sung. It was after she had become the London Idol, with full assurance of the public's loyalty, that she gave us something more than entertainment—something that has direct bearing on life.

At the beginning of the 'nineties she was still singing the praises of those who were "ready at night for a row or a fight," but a little later came "Algy—The Pic-ca-dil-ly John-ny With The Lit-tle Glass Eye." He was as rollicking as his forerunners right until the last line of the last verse when you heard that behind the scenes the girls called him a "jay." Then there arrived the young man named Brown, who went to Paris for a week-end with a fair demoiselle who turned out to be his wife. Once again, you see, Vesta Tilly was telling the story against the masher she mimicked.

Henceforth, instead of merging her own personality into that of the character she acted, she brought her wits to bear upon him critically. By pretending to be young men for so long, she had come to understand them as well as they did themselves. Now she went further, and understood them better than they did themselves. That is why we saw them, not as we could see them in real life but as they were when viewed through a clever woman's eyes.

"By The Sad Sea Waves" illustrated this process. She picked on the poor little London "chappie," earning fifteen shillings a week and spending every penny he could spare on haberdashery for a week at Brighton, where he hoped to pass muster on the promenade as a real masher. Again the story goes against the hero of the song. Back at business, he found that the beauty he met at Brighton was the girl in the cook-shop. No doubt the song-writer had a little mockery in mind. In performance, however, this was magically translated. What we felt when Vesta Tilley showed him to us was not derision but pathos. She felt for him and with him, and her tenderness over

A SONG-FRONT BY ROBERT SEYMOUR, THE FIRST ARTIST TO DRAW MR. PICKWICK

that little scrap of humanity was evident in all the portraits she painted from that time onwards.

Crochety veterans might wonder what on earth the younger generation was coming to, and hold the youths of 1909 up to ridicule in contemptuous sketches (such as the one which appeared that year on the programmes of "An Englishman's Home," at Wyndham's), but Vesta Tilley knew. She knew the heart of the junior clerk as well as she knew the heart of young Tommy Atkins, with his throaty shout of, "Jolly good luck to the girl that loves a soldier"—such a pocket marvel of military precision that nothing of him remained when his place came to be taken by the civilian soldier of the War. No, there was no resemblance whatever between the two. But we recognised the weedy youth in khaki ; we had seen him in "By The Sad Sea Waves." Unknown to the crochety veterans in club arm-chairs, there had always been in him the stuff heroes are made of. He was to win the battles they would do their damnedest to lose. He would man their trenches as cheerfully as he once lined seaside esplan-ade : and the only one to have prophetically recognised it in the past was not he himself—for he died without gaining consciousness that he was a hero—but Vesta Tilley.

Looking back on the junior clerk, we can see how she had dis-cerned pluck even in his drudgery to buy haberdashery. She had always read what was in him. When the time came to answer those cartoons of him as a tailor's dummy with a novelette, she signalised his vindication with, "I joined the Army yesterday, so the Army of to-day's all right." On the surface it was a joke—but only on the surface. As that meagre figure in khaki clumped across the stage in heavy ammunition boots, we might echo Figaro's line which Byron translated in *Don Juan*—"And if I laugh at any mortal thing 'tis that I may not weep."

*   *   *   *   *

When his name was becoming a legend, Arthur Roberts took his farewell of the public at the Alhambra, Leicester Square, in the November of 1924. When he gazed from the stage at the tense, eager crowd that seemed to be bursting a space too small to hold all his admirers, the lump in his throat became swollen. "I don't know," he said, "whether to stand on my head and let it fall out of my mouth or wait till it drops to my feet and then kick it away."

When a bouquet was handed to him, how thoroughly he pulled our legs: "These," he murmured wistfully, "are very beautiful flowers, but I miss the blossom that would remind me most of my youth. It was a flower I was very fond of then." In a voice as smart as the crack of a whip, he added, "Hops!" The pathos in his voice was not merely make-believe. His eyes filled with tears when he asked us to think of him whenever his name was out of the bill, and filled again as quickly as he laughed them away. But his voice soon regained its strength, and with the erect bearing that had always been his and made his jest now sound like a true word, he shouted, "And if anybody wants a juvenile lead in 1925—here I am!"

Unlike most of the other music-hall idols of his time, Arthur Roberts rarely raddled his nose or carried a bulbous "gamp" or wore patched trousers. At one time he was "the glass of fashion and the mould of form," closely watched by all the young bloods for the cut of a coat or the rake of a hat. He always retained his sense of style, and at the Alhambra appeared as an old beau who could still cut a dash. His song, "Good—Damn Good," had the old spirit that once led to his sudden departure from the halls in the past. He was still alert. He could still, with one gesture, picture the whole scene of a story for you.

He was born in London in 1852. At the age of eight he was performing on Yarmouth Sands, and at the age of eighty with the Veterans of Variety. In between these first and last chapters, he spent the 'seventies on the halls, and the 'eighties in pantomime and such burlesque as "The Vicar Of Wideawakefield," "Tra-la-la Tosca," and "Too Lovely Black-Eyed Susan." In the 'nineties he reached his prime as the immaculate Captain Coddington, as Dandy Dan, the Life Guardsman, and as Sir Ormesby St. Leger ("The School Girl"), in the first musical comedies. His experiences in revues ended in a flourish, for at seventy years of age he was engaged by Mr. Cochran as a charioteer in "Phi-Phi" at the London Pavilion. Later on he was regarded with almost incredulous eyes by a new generation which had been brought up to think of him as a legend.

As a link between two distinct generations, he mingled stories of living players with recollections of historic personages in his reminiscences. The scene of the funniest chapter in his *Fifty Years of Spoof* is the Savoy Theatre during the reign of Gilbert and Sullivan. When a charity matinée was being organised, he agreed to be a juryman in "Trial By Jury." The author, who directed rehearsals, besides playing the part of the advocate, bullied the company so unmercifully that Arthur Roberts determined to be revenged :

Very deliberately, having carefully closed the door of the juryman's box, I removed my boots and placed them outside the door. They were a terrible pair of boots, chosen for the occasion, broken, patched and covered with mud. Then, I took a piece of chalk, and bending down, wrote on the outside of the jury box, "Call me at seven."

The music went valiantly on, but the polite buzz of conversation amongst the audience had broken out into an uproar of laughter. Gilbert glared at me and the prawn-like eyebrows appeared to be afflicted with a sudden attack of epilepsy.

I had brought into the juryman's box with me a sombre black bag. This contained whelks. I produced the whelks and solemnly ate them, removing them from the shell with a pin.

After that he twirled the plate on the top of a stick like a juggler. Gilbert gave a signal and a stage-hand beckoned to the offender. But Roberts had not finished yet :

I produced a small beer mug from my pocket, and placed it deliberately on the ledge of the box.

The stage man increased his importunities for me to retire. The opera was in suspension; the audience were in hysterics. I discovered a coin in my pocket, took it out and tossed it in the air.

"Heads I lose!" I ejaculated.

I examined the coin.

"Heads," I exclaimed.

With a sigh, I got up, took hold of the mug, and ambled off the stage with the depressed air of one who has unfortunately been sent to fetch the supper beer.

*   *   *   *   *

"Let's have a song about something to eat and give the girls a rest," was a bright joke early in the reign of George V. "Girls" was then one of the hardest-worked of words. "The Girl Who Took The Wrong Turning" was the favourite drama of simple and sophisticated alike. "The Girls Of Gottenburg" set a fashion at the Gaiety where musical comedies in future all had to be about a girl from somewhere or other. And on the halls Whit Cunliffe, George Lashwood, and Arthur Reece were only three among the many who were singing about "the girls." On the halls it was always *the* girls. "Put me on an island where *the* girls are few," so Wilkie Bard sang, not "where girls are few."

All these singers were popular. Yet both for quality and quantity, Charles Whittle came first. He sang a dozen songs about the girls, and one about "The Girl In The Clogs And Shawl" which deserved to rank as the best of the whole period. Of course, he sang other songs—"We'll All Go The Same Way Home," for one famous example. Not even that, however, caught the public's fancy so surely as "Let's All Go Down The Strand." The singer came from the North, where he had taught himself in the hardest of schools—bar parlours known as "The Spits." Severe critics there thought so much of him that when the evening's programmes were chalked on the mirror over the fireplace he was always "top of the glass."

There was, George Edwardes used to say, magic in the word girl.

GILBERT AND SULLIVAN ("TRIAL BY JURY")

From an "Entr'acte" caricature

Whit Cunliffe was always of the same opinion, from the time he sang "Girls, Girls, Girls" until modern times, when he represented himself to be a colonel who had returned to London after long years of service abroad, only to be bitterly disappointed because the female form divine was no longer plump. Other singers of the halls dressed themselves up as dudes, but few, if any, could look as spruce in grey frockcoat, topper and spats as he did.

With this group the history of mashing comes to its close. Possibly you can trace the cause to Wilkie Bard's song, just mentioned, which ended, "But for goodness' sake don't put me with a Suffragette." The emancipation of women, a stock joke of music-hall comedians for many years, has taken effect. Popular songs about courtship show a very practical frame of mind, whether intentions are honourable or dishonourable. As for the youth who takes an undue interest in his clothes, the names bestowed on him imply that he has no interest either in "the girls" (who now seem to be extinct) or handsome young women.

FIGURES FROM "FOOTLIGHTS"

ARTHUR LLOYD'S GREATEST SUCCESS.
I LIKE TO BE A SWELL
Sung by him nightly with immense applause.

LOST PUPPY

CONCANEN SIEBE & Cᵒ

LITH. 12 FRITH ST SOHO W.

FOR I LIKE TO BE A SWELL   OR ANYWHERE I DONT MUCH CARE
TO WALK ALONG PALL MALL   SO I CAN BE A SWELL
WRITTEN AND COMPOSED BY
GASTON MURRAY

ENT. STA. HALL   PRICE 3/-

66 AN ARTHUR LLOYD SONG-FRONT

CHAPTER NINE

Ballads of Drama

In the modern music-hall the dramatic ballad is dead. Managements of to-day deprive us of the chance to hear the few "descriptive vocalists" that are left. They are only engaged when some attempt is made to revive the atmosphere of the old halls. But we do not need long memories to bear Tom Costello and George Lashwood in mind. Nor, although he died in 1900, has Charles Godfrey been forgotten; there are many who fondly recall his songs and the elaborately-staged sketches which provided them with a setting of fights for the flag.

That there was another side to his character is evident in his other songs about "going on the spree," right back to his "Masher King" of the early 'eighties in silk knee-breeches and buckled shoes, and his "Oh! For The Jubilee" tippler in 1887. He was as famous for these bursts of revelry, each with its climax of knocking policemen down and taking the consequences, as he was for his appearance in uniform. Though "Hi-Tiddley-Hi-Ti" was the most popular—it had to be followed by a "companion-song" called "Regent Street" recording a similar pilgrim's progress—he sang many of them.

There was more in him than the sharp contrast of revelry in the West and heroism at the front or on the sea. He could combine the two in one song, as he did in "Seeing Life," which began with champagne bubbles and ended with storm billows. In addition, he could be the Giddy Little Curate, the grandfather at his own birthday party, the henpecked husband, the gallant in the omnibus, a dumbshow pierrot inspired by the success of that famous wordless play, "L'Enfant Prodigue," the Regency buck in "The Good Old Times," and the irate German father of "Jacob Strauss." He had a large repertory of his own songs to match such versatility, but he would also prove his worth by picking a ballad chosen by his rivals. "After The Ball" had many singers, including Vesta Tilley. But when I bracketed it with her name in a radio programme, many listeners reproached me for not associating it with Charles Godfrey.

Few music-hall comedians had such success with songs of so definitely a tragic nature as "The Lost Daughter" or "Across The Bridge," which had plots about desperate suicides. Contrast these with the frivolous nonsense of "Will You Be Mine, Pretty Bird," and then think of "Siberia," "Here Upon Guard Am I," "The Last Shot," and "The Royal Fusiliers." In these his early training in melodrama, under his own name of Paul Lacey at the Pavilion Theatre in the East End, was manifest.

In *Idols of the Halls*, Chance Newton describes the excitement when, in "On Guard," Godfrey appeared as "a starving old tramp warrior" and asked for a night's shelter at the workhouse casual ward.

"Be off, you tramp!" said the janitor. "You are not wanted here!"

"No!" thundered the tattered veteran. "I am not wanted *here*. But at Balaklava—I was wanted *there*!"

Godfrey, who would study night and day to make his impersonations of Nelson, Drake, and Gordon exact in detail, was so careless in other ways that when he arrived at a music-hall after a walk through London, messengers had to be sent back to "every house of call" on the way to collect his band parts. Chance Newton says that after a voyage to Australia for his health, Godfrey came back worse than he went, "thanks to the foolish 'hospitality' out there, and on the out and home voyages." He died at the age of forty-nine while trying to fulfil an engagement at Birmingham.

Our last memories of him consist mainly of gunpowder. His military sketch, "Balaclava," by Wal Pink, concluded "with a magnificent Tableau ('Into The Jaws Of Death') representing the famous Charge of the Six Hundred." There was a resounding stage battle in which the hero's horse was shot under him, and the next turn had to come on before the clouds of smoke had rolled away. One week this next turn was a sentimental tenor. He coughed and spluttered so much in the aftermath of fireworks that the audience laughed more joyfully at him than at the programme's star comedian.

*   *   *   *   *

"The Kipling of the Music-Halls," Leo Dryden might be called. Among all the many singers of patriotic songs, he was the foremost Imperialist. The Legion of Frontiersmen welcomed him into their ranks as a tribute to his pioneering to remote parts of the British Empire—in spirit. The compliment would have been deserved if he had become famous for "The Miner's Dream Of Home" alone. Fortune has not been kind to him in recent years; in fact he felt compelled to sing in streets at one time to make it known that he was still alive. But we cannot yet foresee the time when the best of his songs will be forgotten.

George Dryden Wheeler is his real name. He was born on June 6, 1863, in London, and began life as an engineer. He was also a printer for a time. Meanwhile he was preparing for his destiny as an amateur in a minstrel troupe. At eighteen years of age he took the plunge as a turn at the Foresters in Cambridge Road, Whitechapel, where he came under the influence of Charles Godfrey's stirring spectacle,

COLONEL NEWCOME STALKS OUT OF THE CAVE OF HARMONY
From Richard Doyle's illustration to "The Newcomes"

"On Guard." After eight years' steady endeavour, Leo Dryden made his name with "Love And Duty" and "The Miner's Dream Of Home." He was part author of these, and both author and composer of some of his later ballads, notably "Bravo, Dublin Fusiliers," which Pat Rafferty also sang.

After representing Australians in his red shirt and slouch hat, Leo Dryden hymned the praises of South Africans in "What Britishers Are Made Of," and Canadian Redskins in "Great White Mother." Still more inspiriting was his appearance as a Rajah in "India's Reply," which echoed through streets and country lanes. "The Gallant Gordon Highlanders" was another triumph. These were the rage all the year round throughout the Boer War. Family parties romped to them, errand boys whistled them, pierrot troupes sang them, buskers with portable harmoniums played them, and they were the climax of spectacles in Christmas pantomimes. Nowadays the wedding of principal boy and principal girl may be celebrated amid allegorical tableaux of seaside resorts or city guilds to excite municipal pride and thus avert—vain hopes—an anti-climax. But from 1899 to 1901 (and later) the most rousing moments in the traditionally dramatised fairy-tale always occurred when the grand pageantry of the finale grouped itself around the standing figure of a towering Britannia.

Khaki was the favourite colour everywhere, as Marie Lloyd told us in a song about the popularity of khaki shirts and khaki skirts when she dressed herself up like a female C.I.V. Pantomime choruses might wear rainbow hues in early scenes, but in the last they had to wear, and were proud to wear, the uniforms of all the soldiers of the Empire—New Zealand Lancers, Cape Town Highlanders, and North-West Mounted Police—in a grand ballet after the manner of an assault-at-arms. How stirring such sights were! How we cheered when the medallion just above Britannia's head changed into a white sheet upon which magic-lanterns projected the portraits of Buller, Baden-Powell, French, White, Kitchener and "Bobs"! Those were great pantomime days, for war, though long-drawn out, was remote and therefore romantic. When Dick Whittington, after saying farewell to Alice Fitzwarren, had the stage to him (her) self in order to sing, "Good-bye, Dolly, I Must Leave You," it did not strike us as incongruous even though our own father had just left for the Emergency Camp at Aldershot.

There were passions to be roused in the public breast in those days and Leo Dryden knew how to rouse them nobly. Yet the romantic singer of "India's Reply" could doff his picturesque garb in a trice and appear the next moment as a dude, in topper and boiled shirt, to sing about beer and mothers-in-law in, "Take No Notice." No wonder he was as well known at the beginning of this century as the heroes of Mafeking and Kimberley! And yet before many years had passed the nature of variety had so changed that his engagements became less and less frequent. Shortly after *the* War his position became so difficult that he decided to go direct to

69, 70 BALLADS OF DRAMA FROM OUTPOSTS OF EMPIRE

the public since he lacked the chance to have the public brought to him.

Handbills were pushed through letter-boxes, announcing the times of his performances in the street. He had never known stage-fright in his career. But now he had a sudden and acute attack of street-fright. Wearing his old astrachan coat he kept to his engagements, singing hour after hour until ten o'clock at night. His takings were elevenpence. At the next attempt his rewards improved, although his coat and the telephone number on his handbills, as well as his declaration that he was not a starving beggar but merely a music-hall "star" using a pitch instead of a stage, did not help the collection.

In the nick of time he was enlisted for the first troupe of "Veterans Of Variety." At all the halls they visited, "The Miner's Dream Of Home" was the greatest hit of the evening. But his luck was out again in 1925 when he told the judge at the Westminster County Court, "I am on my beam ends. The music-hall profession is in a precarious position." Since then he has revisited such glimpses of his prime as the Star, Bermondsey, and more recently we saw him as a chairman at Collins's, Islington Green. There we cheered him as the creator of what will always rank, no matter how fashions in entertainments may change, among music-hall "classics."

★　★　★　★　★

If the title of *lion comique* has ever been deserved it is by Tom Costello. In the dramatic vein he is a lion; in the comic he has been among the first as dude, tramp or dame. "The most versatile artist of the halls," is the praise such excellent judges as Charles Austin ("Parker, P.C.") have bestowed upon him.

From Birmingham, where he was born in 1863, Tom Costello went to Wolverhampton to make his start on the stage; he arrived in London at the age of twenty-three to play a comic Mephistopheles in one of George Conquest's pantomimes at the old Surrey (now pulled down to make way for the new wing of a hospital). "Comrades" definitely set him among the stars. Who will forget his forthright gesture as the cavalryman, in service grey shirt with braces hanging over the crimson trousers of his "Cherry Pickers" Hussar uniform, in the tale of a last good-bye on the battlefield? Now turn from this memory to that of him as the henpecked husband in "At Trinity Church" with a stump on one leg and the hip of the other standing out like a bustle, or as the red-nosed "fair charmer" of "Who's Going To Mash Me To-night?"

At one time he was famous for his hoaxes. While singing about his desire to murder the originator of the phrase, "There's 'Air," he declared he would shoot the next one to say it. When a dandy in

M 2

the stage-box immediately did so, Costello "shot" him and the supposed corpse was carried out through the audience. He shouted, "Come up here on the stage," to a heckler, who accepted the challenge and presented a writ : no one in the audience knew at the time who was hoaxed or who was hoaxing.

*   *   *   *   *

George Lashwood is numbered among the singers of "girl" songs by virtue of "There's A Girl Wanted Here," but what distinguishes him from the others in this group is his resemblance to the *lions comiques*. Like Leybourne and Vance, he can change from light comedy to broad fun, and from sentiment to drama. That was apparent at the very beginning of his career. After six years in the provinces he came to London in the summer of 1899, working Gatti's-Under-The Arches, Gatti's-In-The-Road, and the "Old Mo" the same night, with "The Last Bullet," "The Tipster," and "My Poll." His military and patriotic ballads are almost as well known as his light-hearted ditties.

Then there is George Leyton. That so very British a singer should have been born in New Orleans is a most surprising fact. At twenty-five he was an actor in London, taking part in "True Heart" at the Princess's in the summer of 1889 and singing the song from which the play took its name. His first variety engagement was at the Royal (formerly Weston's and later the Holborn Empire) in March, 1910, whence he went to sing "The Emigrant Ship" at the Trocadero. Of all his songs in uniform, "Boys Of The Chelsea School" is rightly the most famous. He sang it in the past to raise funds for survivors of the Crimea and the Indian Mutiny; and it was as stirring when he sang it again after a war that had been re-markable (among other things) for inspiring no popular ballads in the heroic style.

CHAPTER TEN

Round About Leicester Square

WHEN the lorry in Leicester Square turned sharply and drove through the façade of the Alhambra, the effect was like the beginning of a sequel to *Through the Looking Glass*. Nor did that feeling vanish when the cart-track (where the box office had been) led to a rubbish heap where gold stars dragged down from the ceiling twinkled in pallid daylight. Through the skeleton of the dome a Moorish turret showed. This time the threat to turn the Alhambra into a picture theatre had to be taken seriously.

Once more the Empire, which had suffered this fate in 1926, and the Alhambra, were to be rivals—with films. In the past it was with dancers whose pirouettes and entrechats gave glamour to the name of Leicester Square. There was no "art" about ballet then : its poetry of motion attempted to express nothing without the aid of dialogue, songs, show girls, and booted, even trousered, supers. Yet it never lacked good dancers, even though the "shapely and handsomely dressed women" did make their silk tights flash for the delight of houses where "gentlemen rather than ladies were the best patrons."

Around the little bar in the corner of the Empire promenade or on its velvet couches, in the reek of mingled Jockey Club and cigar smoke, a tale used to be told which many who said they knew the youth who was the chief character in it, believed. He had left the Empire with one of the women of the promenade, stayed the night in her room, happened to open a wardrobe—and saw the body there of a man in evening dress with a knife thrust through the shirt-front.

After hurrying from the house in a long search for a constable, the youth forgot which way he had come. That was the account he gave at the Empire. There one night he exclaimed, "That's the girl." She recognised him and ran. He pursued her with two or three of his friends not far behind. They saw him turn into Lisle Street. When they came to the corner, he had vanished. They never saw him again.

To my mind then the women of the promenade were dull and humdrum compared to the corps de ballet. Why I liked the place was because of the mellow Victorians who exchanged memories and were glad to find you listening. While courtesans paraded all the way from Cranbourn Street to Hyde Park Corner, you took as little notice of them as you did of policemen. Outcries against the vice of the promenade seemed justified only when I became aware one night that a young French woman next to me in the crush round the bar, had left off her corsets. All this suggests now is that she had anticipated the general fashion by a few years. Then it was scandalous behaviour.

With or without reformers, Leicester Square has always changed. Once it was a lordly place, dominated on the north side by Leicester House which was called "the pouting place of princes" because twice an heir apparent who had quarrelled with his royal father went to live there. While George III, as a prince, was finishing his studies in a house on the east side, he was brought, from a carnival at Venice, a

THE EMPIRE PROMENADE
From a drawing by Will Owen

model of *Le Tableau Mouvant*, "the scenes being painted as transparencies, and the figures being all black profiles." A Moorish palace first arose on the east side in 1854 when Victorian godparents, armed with a Royal charter, christened it the Royal Panopticon and dedicated it "to assist by moral and intellectual agencies, the best interests of society." Waxworks were tried next, but these, like all else, failed. At public auction the Panopticon went for a few thousands to E. T. Smith, formerly a Bow Street runner, who was the most reckless theatrical speculator of his day. After clearing away the diving apparatus, the new "ascending carriage" (a lift), and the fountain of coloured water, he obtained a music, dancing, drinking and smoking licence for his "Alhambra Palace." Almost immediately it passed out of his hands into those of Howes and Cushing for their American Circus. When that departed he restored the music-hall licence and "the cooking and culinary apparatus." The audience sat at tables and were served with oysters, steaks, chops and stewed cheese, besides liquors which included "mouth tickler," "stone fence," and "locomotive," prepared by an "expressly engaged" American. Leotard,

73 THE ANIMATOGRAPHE—BEGINNING OF THE END—BILLED AT THE ALHAMBRA IN 1895

From a photograph by Paul Martin

74 AUDITORIUM OF THE ALHAMBRA, NOVEMBER 1936

Central Press

"the daring young man on the flying trapeze," was paid £180 a week to fly through the air over the tables with no net beneath him, until

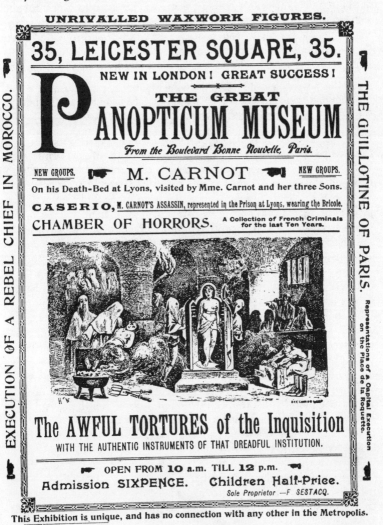

A WAX-WORKS HAND-BILL

he returned to France, where he died of small-pox at the age of twenty-eight.

There was a grand orchestra of over sixty, and a company of over four hundred performers appeared in grand spectacular ballets.

Madame Pitteri, the "première danseuse assoluta," was famous for the new idea of dyeing her hair to a "beautiful gold," for her richly-appointed dressing-room with a toilette service of solid silver, for the rich presents princes bestowed upon her, for her daily bath in warm milk, and for her lavish generosity. She was beloved by all. When the Alhambra ballet called "The Spirit Of The Deep" was transferred to Paris, she went with it. Years later news of her death came to London:

Died in poverty and distress; died while filling an engagement in a low dancing-house among the sailors at Marseilles. She had spent all her money; the presents were gone, so were the princes.

In one of the Alhambra ballets of her time, ninety girls were clamped in irons to the scenery from the stage-level to the flies. While they were fixed in these positions one night, a cigarette which had been dropped through a grating in the promenade set light to packing-cases in the cellar. Smoke began to rise into the auditorium. The girls thought the theatre was on fire and half of them fainted. The scene was changed at top speed and they were all brought down without mishap, mainly because the straw in the packing-cases was damp.

Leicester Square's centre was occupied from 1851 to 1861 by an educational entertainment called "Wylde's Globe." When it was removed, the site became a howling wilderness, surrounding an equestrian statue of George I which was beginning to shed its limbs. One night a treasonable plot was hatched against it. While the attention of the police force was drawn to another quarter, an expedition set out from the scene-painters' store of the Alhambra armed with pots and props. The next morning all the inhabitants of the Square looked out on what they termed an outrage. George I wore a dunce's cap. His face was decorated with a beard, and he was armed with a long pole topped by a birch broom. His horse had been painted white with black spots all over it like a rocking-horse. After that George I was removed and only the horse remained in a sea of brickbats and refuse.

Towards the close of the 'sixties Finette brought the Can-Can from Paris to the Alhambra. Next came the Colonna Quadrille, which included a wispy slip of a girl named Sarah Wright who had very short skirts and very long legs. The verb "to kick," said Emily Soldene, "had never been so actively conjugated before," and the Middlesex magistrates were so horrified that they took away the Alhambra's licence. As "The Parisian Quadrille," the troupe was engaged by Emily Soldene at the Philharmonic, Islington. Sarah Wright (billed as "Mdlle. Sara" in imitation of Sara Bernhardt), now "kicked up her agile heels a little higher than had previously been deemed possible and was equally successful in dusting the floor with

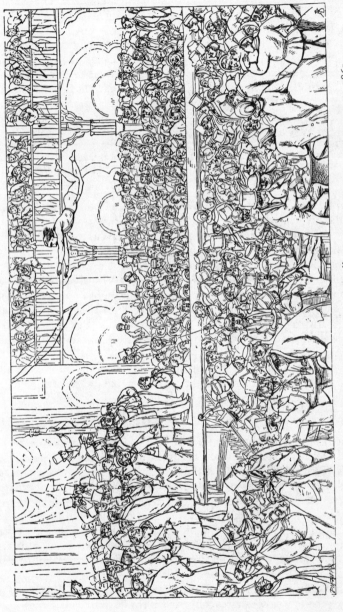

"THAT DARING YOUNG MAN ON THE FLYING TRAPEZE": LEOTARD AT THE ALHAMBRA IN 1861
From a drawing by Richard Doyle

95

her back hair." The theatre was crammed, and "Sara The Kicker, Wiry Sal," became the toast of the London clubs. "Piccadilly Jim" (Sir James Farquharson) was the only doubter. When asked, "Isn't she wonderful?" he answered, "Umph! Yes, but I was thinking of her people. It must be very disagreeable to have anyone belonging to you gifted like that." As for Finette, she went to the Near East, lost her money and her health, and died in a hospital at Constantinople.

For a while the Alhambra was restricted to promenade concerts. But these were far from sedate. On the outbreak of the Franco-Prussian War, each performance wound up with

THE WAR SONGS OF THE DAY

1st. The Watch on the Rhine.	3rd. The Marseillaise.
2nd. Garibaldi's Hymn.	4th. Rule Britannia.

Item 1 was the signal for the Germans to cheer; they were attacked by the French, who raised counter cheers at Item 3, when the singer, half enveloped in the Tricolour, fell on her knees as though in prayer. While the battle was raging, the roughs of Seven Dials would steal in to pick pockets and help themselves to drinks. The Kangaroo, a gigantic negro prize-fighter, was the ringleader. Even the patriots stopped their fight when he was opposed one night by a man half his size and knocked out, after which he was never seen again. Meanwhile hatters and umbrella-makers prospered. Bits of umbrellas and walking-sticks and battered hats, were swept up each night from all parts of the house.

In the April of 1871 the Alhambra shook off the control of the magistrates by opening as a theatre under the Lord Chamberlain. English opera was tried before the long run of Offenbach's "Le Roi Carotte," from the June of 1872, began the brilliant reign of *opéra bouffe* with ballet as its consort. The next year the management pulled a snook at the magistrates, for Mdlle. Sara led the quadrille in "La Belle Hélène." Trouble occurred of a different kind. Supporters of Paris (Rose Bell) unjustly and unwarrantably hissed Hélène (Kate Santley) night after night, until summoned to appear at Marlborough Street on a charge of conspiracy. After ten years of melodious nights, the Alhambra went up in flames. There was a deafening crash when the circles collapsed, and some of the firemen lost their lives. It was a bitter night in December, and water from the hoses became frozen so that what had been a Moorish palace looked the next morning like a Russian palace with its façade of icicles.

The "Alhambra Theatre Royal" which opened on December 3, 1883, graced a new square, converted from "a filthy wilderness into a blooming garden and a thing of beauty" by Baron Albert Grant, M.P., a company promoter. During a temporary spell of prosperity,

75 "THE KANGAROO" VISITS THE ALHAMBRA

From "London in the Sixties" by
"One of the Old Brigade," London, 1907

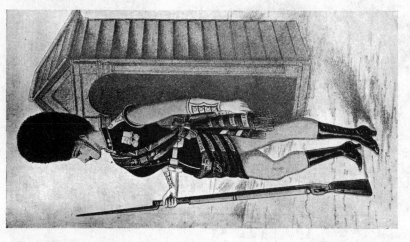

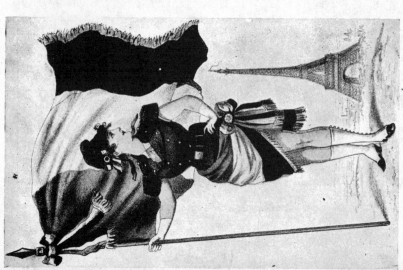

76, 77, 78 COSTUME DESIGNS FOR THE GRAND SPECTACLE OF "OUR ARMY AND NAVY"
AT THE ALHAMBRA IN THE 'NINETIES

he bought the site, planted trees, laid out flower-beds, erected the statue to Shakespeare, set up the four busts in honour of local genius, and signed a deed of transfer to the Metropolitan Board of Works, before vanishing from our story while fortune was vanishing from his. All his "improvements" were of so little help to the Alhambra at first that it had to drop the imposture of being a theatre royal, and re-opened as the Alhambra Theatre of Varieties in 1884. Across the Square in the April of that year the Empire began life as a theatre. Three years later it changed into a music-hall, and Leicester Square began the chapter of its existence which now seems almost legendary. Both houses became temples of that type of ballet in which almost anything was translated in terms of pretty girls. One night the *corps de ballet* would personify the Armies of All Nations. Another night they would be All the Ingredients of a Salad, not forgetting the mustard-pot and slices of hard-boiled egg. Fleet Street ought to have felt flattered when the subject was "The Press," for newspapers have never seemed so elegant, graceful and alluring as when brought to life at the Empire in this manner. That was the old Leicester Square's mission in life. It tried to teach us how to see reality with a tinge of glamour. Perhaps you may remember Max Beerbohm's comment on a Covent Garden market scene in the ballet. "Covent Garden," he said, "is not at all like that—but don't you wish it were."

There were also stars in the variety half of the programme. In the year of the Diamond Jubilee the leading light of the Alhambra was Cissie Loftus, at the height of her career as a mimic which was the prelude to successes in comic opera, in Shakespeare under Irving, in "Peter Pan," in Ibsen and in Hollywood. "And you, Cissie Loftus, my first and charming imitator, who came and asked me to help you to parody me! You must admit that I was very obliging!" So Yvette Guilbert writes in *The Song of My Life*, after describing her own triumph at the Empire in 1894, three years after her long black gloves and "that neck unique in its proportions and shape" had become famous in Paris at the Divan Japonais.

As the 'nineties ended, the Alhambra became the magnet for stars from all over the world—from Australia a soubrette or two; from America, lady cyclists and sopranos; from the Continent, Fregoli, the Protean, who played eight out of nine parts in one play, and Charmion, the daring young woman on the trapeze, as well as dancers and singers of all countries for the two ballets given each night. Two Spanish stars outshone all. One was Senorita Consuelo Torta-jada who sang and danced at the Alhambra for many months. The other, still more renowned, was La Belle Otero, who is now living in the South of France, after blazing her trail from one of the world's great capitals to another, and recording it in *My Story*, which stakes

N

a claim to be considered first among autobiographies for sheer candour. At the Palais de Crystal, Marseilles, she had been hissed nightly for a fortnight. The leader of the *claque* confessed that he was in the pay of her rival, who had been jilted and considered Otero to blame. One night the stars met :

Felicia rose hastily, and dragged a hat-pin out of her hat as if she were seizing the nearest weapon. Seeing my enemy ready for the fray, caring nothing for my own possible blinding or disfigurement, I was quicker of movement than she. I seized the chair she had been sitting on, and struck her on the shoulder so heavily that she fell. It was an iron chair, such as you find in public gardens, and the blow must have been a hard one. Felicia began to howl aloud. When I saw her on the ground, I sprang forward, and would have thrown myself upon her like a veritable savage. . . .

In Russia a wealthy sheep farmer attacked her. She "seized hold of everything in the room that could help me" until he took fright, "seeing the sheer frenzy I was in, and crawled for protection under the supper table." She went to the chief of police, who was "most affable and kind and . . . enterprising." Though she had only gone to him to lodge a complaint, her visit "lasted four days."

. At first the new century brought little change, and the Dresden delicacy of Genée, at the Empire from 1897 until 1907, remained the delight of Leicester Square. The years of revolution in London entertainment were from 1910 to 1912. Amusement seekers then had an intensive education in the new "Three R's"—Ragtime, Revue, and Russian Ballet. Between them they drove *the ballet* from its temples, though not at once for first Kyasht and then Bedells stepped into Genée's empty shoes, and Britta came to the Alhambra. Enrico Cecchetti's Imperial Ballet danced "Le Lac des Cygnes" at the Hippodrome ; Karsavina was at the Coliseum, and Anna Pavlova with Mordkin at the Palace. Ballet was restored to the opera house next year, when Diaghileff presented Karsavina and Nijinsky at Covent Garden, and no longer belonged to the halls. Ragtime (brought to the Palace in 1912 by the American Ragtime Octette) joined forces with revue to create "Kill That Fly" at the Alhambra, and "Everybody's Doing It" at the Empire—titles that indicate the prevailing taste.

It was at this time that Gaby Deslys first came to Leicester Square, after playing a part in the overthrow of the Portuguese monarchy. When the assassinations were being plotted, public unrest was fanned by accounts of the wealth bestowed on her and of the price paid for her "ropes of pearls." When fanatics rushed the palace and killed the king, her life might have been taken had she not escaped from the city by hiding in a hay-cart. She came back to London where she had previously appeared at the Gaiety as the Charm of Paris. Now

80 OTERO

79 LA TORTAJADA

81, 82 GABY DESLYS—BEFORE AND AFTER SHE ACQUIRED THE PEARLS

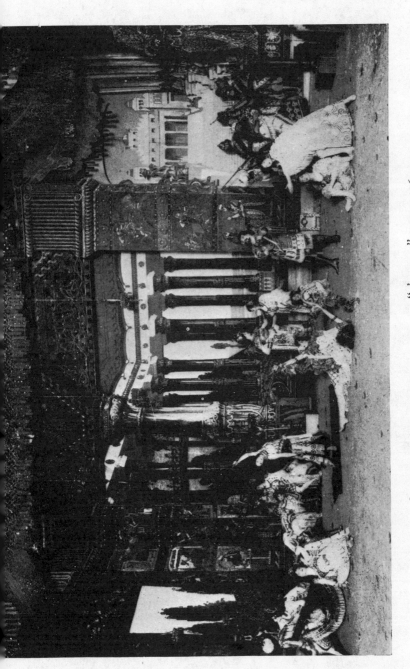

83 SCENE FROM THE ALHAMBRA BALLET, "L'AMOUR," JUNE, 1906

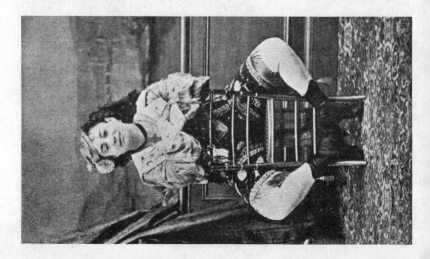

THE EMPIRE BALLET OF "DOLLY"

From "The Illustrated Sporting and Dramatic News," Jan. 3, 1891

with a legend around her name as well as those pearls around her neck, she became a star at the Alhambra in the year of the revolution in Portugal when the republic was proclaimed after battle and siege in Lisbon.   During the War, when she was at the Alhambra in "5064 Gerrard," she seemed to embody the reckless gaiety of that London of dark streets, air raids, and soldiers from the three corners of the earth.   She had so flamboyant a way with her that she acted the same part on the stage and off.   Everything about her, from her pearls and huge fans to the white car she drove continually despite petrol restrictions, caught the public eye.   Her enemies added to the effect by sending roughs to throw pennies on the stage when she was at the Globe Theatre; one of them held so desperately that he could not be dragged from the dress-circle by four men until the manager, Mr. MacQueen-Pope, brought an ebony ruler hard down upon his wrists.

Gaby Deslys' manner was disarmingly frank, especially when she turned earnestly towards you with a childlike look, and though she had earned a reputation for being mercenary through and through, a sense of mischief might impel her to flaunt her bewitchments upon some old, dry, hard-headed business man during a trifling debate over her theatrical concerns, and leave him bewildered.   She quarrelled in her love affairs and could blaze into picturesque fits of bad temper. Away from this side of her life she inspired strong liking even among those who did not admire her stage performances—her fixed smile, her dancing that was mainly posing, and her little cries that suggested a dulcet parrot.   With her it was the legend that mattered.   Her death from cancer of the throat in 1920, when she was thirty-six years of age, marked the end of London's belief in such feminine glamour and the beginning of the period of disenchantment.

Leicester Square's old spirit was vanishing.   There was an outcry against the promenades and they were "closed," a social reform achieved by refusing to let women loiter there, as though the whole sex was a contamination.   What had been hailed by the moralists as a measure of modern enlightenment soon became regarded as the relic of a barbarous age.   At the Alhambra one night, two old ladies tried to buy "rover tickets" for the ballet after all seats had been sold. The manager told them they were not allowed to stand, and when they thought he considered them infirm, he tried to explain but could not: the rule that the promenade was forbidden ground for females had become preposterous in the century of women's rights.

87, 88 PERFORMERS IN THE ALHAMBRA BALLET, "PARISIANA," DECEMBER, 1905

CHAPTER ELEVEN

Scots

SCOTS who take to the halls start with an advantage. Possessed of a national character that is notoriously contrary, they are born with the flavour of comedy in their mouths. Being as generous as they are mean, as open-hearted as they are close-fisted, as humorous as they are dour, they create laughter naturally. All their traditions mingle glamour and mockery. Even the haggis has a little of the romance that belongs to the heather and the kilt, and nothing will destroy the glory of the bagpipes, not even the story that "the Irish sent them over to the Scots who have not yet seen the joke." When Sir Harry Lauder attributes his success to "Scottish grit," the same incongruity becomes evident. Though much to be admired, grit is not so rare as the golden gift of song. His world-wide popularity is not due simply to his efforts, but to the spark of Burns' fire he inherited at birth. Perhaps I could not describe Lauder as a poet without making you smile, but I can confidently assert that he is half-poet, half-comedian. There never has been before, and probably never will be again, such a hybrid. Yet from the way he talks you would think his power over hearts came not from Heaven but from his own pugnacity. Plenty of people have grit—it's the gold that is so scarce. In his songs you will catch its gleams, faint but still there. At the first glance there may be no resemblance between the lyric beginning "She's a winsome wee thing" and "She's Ma Daisy"; at the second you see what they have in common is that the lines sing themselves. Often enough the sense of Lauder's songs is awkward, but they always suggest effortless ease. Hear the chorus once and it remains in your ears for ever. "I Love A Lassie," "I Love My Jean," "I Know A Lassie Out In Ohio," are as spontaneous as love at first sight.

Then consider Lauder's power of living a song. Of all his ditties, only "She's Ma Daisy" fails in this respect. For this number he wears a fantastic uniform, including spurred jack-boots and kilt. It is funny merely in a conventional way, and the patter belongs strictly to the music-hall. But his Highland lovers bring the scent of the heather across the footlights, even though no lover expressed his ecstasy in such comic dancing, though no dandy attired himself like these, though no love-sick eyes ever mistook a rabbit for the lassie who was

101

the apple of them.   Nature seems to have intended him for caricature, for his face is magnified, and his body, with short thick legs and tiny squat feet, diminished.   Nature was subtle when she framed him, but he is subtle too.   Nobody has had time yet to write a disquisition on his skill in make-up, but not for lack of material.   For every song he seems to have a distinct complexion.   Compare the blooming cheeks of the exuberant dandy in kilts, hugging himself with joy at the thought of his lassie, with the sagging skin and shadowed eyes of the old married man, jubilantly setting out for a holiday because his wife is in hospital and himself "off the chain."   Note the different ways they tie their ties or shoe their feet.   When he is a soldier he has a weather-beaten appearance, and when a town loafer there is a sedentary look in his face.

This is but the beginning of his powers of studying and simulating "character."   Each Highland lover, and he has quite a stock of them, is distinct.   Best of all is the one who courts "Mary, My Scotch Bluebell."   What eagerness there is in his pose as he waits for her, one foot in the air, head running away from his body with eagerness, and the stick not daring to touch the ground in case this should delay his rush to meet her directly she shall appear.   The lover whose lass is in Ohio has no such immediate hopes.   His tenderness is expressed in a dance that acts as a safety-valve for his soul's impatience.   Every one of these lovers has his own particular dance, though all the dances are of the ecstatic kind, just as each has his own stick, though all the sticks are of the curly kind.   Now, to get the range of Lauder's contrasts, think of the loafer in trousers who sings, "It's nice to get up in the morning, but it's nicer to lie in your bed."   Here is a type we have all met at times—the stranger who sidles up to you and talks as if you were his lifelong friend.   In the patter of this song, you recognise the supernatural conviction in that stranger's way of laying down the law upon matters of not the slightest consequence.

Lauder has met all types in the course of his varied life.   His father was a trainer for athletics, who chose a wife from the Black Isle, Ross-shire ; they made their home in Portobello, a dingy suburb of Edinburgh, and there Harry Lauder was born.   At the age of eleven he went to a flax-mill at Arbroath, Forfarshire, where he was paid two shillings a week for working half-time.   In odd hours he was educated by a schoolmaster he always refers to as "Stumpy Bill," whose task was not easy.   All the energy the boy might have given to reading, writing, and arithmetic, he put into winning a watch that was the prize at a singing competition for amateurs in the village hall.

In a coal-mine at Hamilton he had to look after pit-ponies—ten years later he went to the House of Commons to ask support for a

clause for their welfare in the Coal Mines Bill. As a full-fledged
miner he sometimes stood up to the hips in water, swinging a pick
at the coal over his head. Because he sang at his work, his powers
as an entertainer became so much talked about that offers of as much
as five shillings were made to him to appear at local concerts. He
transformed himself into a real professional by joining a concert party
at Lanark. His first engagement as a single turn was at Belfast, where
he sang an Irish song called "Calligan, Call Again."

In the May of 1900, when thirty years of age, he came to Gatti's
Theatre of Varieties, Westminster Bridge Road, a humble little affair
with a tiny stage, only two dressing-rooms, and "limes" hung on
the wall. How he seized the chance has been told by Bransby Williams
who was acting Barnaby Rudge at the Tivoli, where Bessie Bonehill,
male impersonator, was billed but could not appear through illness.
In the hunt for a deputy, the Scottish comedian at Gatti's was discovered. But his name was not announced, and the time fixed for
his turn clashed with the time he was to appear at Gatti's:

Poor Harry was in a bit of a quandary. He was wandering about the
landings outside the dressing-rooms, props. in an old carpet bag, a curious
mixture of hope and depression on his face, when I learned of his predicament.
I had been through the mill myself, and I sympathised with him. I volun-
teered to stand down for a turn so that he could get on and off the sooner.
Very gladly he accepted my offer. He went on and his first song was "Lass
O' Tobermory." The audience positively went frantic about him.

In response to the applause, he "promptly scandalised tradition,
Tivoli etiquette, and everything else bound to red tape." While the
manager stood gesticulating frantically in the wings, he usurped the
privilege solely accorded to stars of established reputation, by making
a speech. Afterwards, when the manager said, "You'll never come
on this stage again," he answered, "Some day you may be ver-ra
glad to have me here."

Taking his tone from the manager, the luggage-man refused to
carry the comedian's carpet-bag to the ancient brougham which was
to travel across Westminster Bridge. The cabby whipped up his
horse. It started suddenly, snatched the shafts clean away from the
cab, and bolted, "leaving an amazed and swearing cabby on the box
and an astonished comedian in the lurch." Thus began the career of
one who (long before he was knighted in 1919 for his services in
organising charity concerts during the War), earned the highest
income on the halls, if not in the whole of the entertainment world.

If "being Scotch" were a religion, he would make converts by the
thousands. You cannot escape the evangelical side of his character.
Sooner or later in the evening he will boldly announce his belief in

temperance, thrift, pugnacity and grit, his homely face shining with
the sweat of ecstasy as he sings that desperate ballad about keeping
right on to the end of the road. Like a Salvationist of the sect of
Samuel Smiles and "Self Help," he will force his fervour upon the
audience until they join in the chorus with hushed voices and awed
faces. Into this he puts his whole heart, and you begin to doubt
whether he knows the whys and wherefores of his success. What he
has set out to do, he says, is to give the public "healthy, innocent
entertainment," and he adds, "I've succeeded admirably." Would
any other celebrity of the halls be content with purely negative praise?
In the same talk he tells the tale of the American lost in Aberdeen
who wanted to know the way, was asked, "Is there a reward offered
for ye?" answered "Not yet," and was told "Then you're still lost."
That goes against himself when he says, "Tell your friends I'm here.
I'm spending no more money on advertising." There is no doubt
that he enjoys these jokes about his meanness; yet, when a laughing
voice from the stalls says, "Scotch," he fervently declares, "Yes,
thank God, I'll never be anything else." Although this is beside the
point—for he has only himself to blame—the audience applauds him
as a martyr. Still, the singer of "I Love A Lassie" may blether if
he wants to.

*   *   *   *   *

For over sixty years Charles Whitton McCullum has been known
to the public as Charlie Coburn. For just on fifty of them he has
been singing "Two Lovely Black Eyes." Make no mistake about
it, the success of that song was no mere accident. At first it was
nothing more than a vague idea in his mind that "My Nelly's Blue
Eyes" of the Christy Minstrels ought to be parodied. Next came a
determination to rewrite it comically. After that came the struggle,
for such it was to him no matter how simple the words may seem
now, of poetic composition. Nothing short of inspiration was
needed to supply "Oh, what a surprise!" as the second line to avoid
"Two lovely black eyes" thrice in each chorus. All this is in his
autobiography, where he confesses how he applied for his engagement
at the Trocadero (in the summer of 1866) while the too-critical
manager was away:

> My turn was something after ten o'clock and I well remember how dear
> old Pony Moore, Gene Stratton, Sam Raeburn and others—members of the
> Moore and Burgess Minstrels at St. James's Hall near by—would come in
> every night, after they had done their work, and sit in the stalls and help me
> loyally with the chorus. On some nights they would seem to be almost
> the only people in the hall.

By working "the chorus for all its was worth," he had his reward in less than a fortnight. Audiences came in simply to join in the chorus. One reveller who sang it right through the entire programme and was afterwards knocked down outside, continued it in the gutter. As doors and windows were open because of the heat, massed voices from the Trocadero were wafted across Great Windmill Street to the London Pavilion, where the audience stopped their own show in order to take part. Titled "swells" at the tables in the side saloon caught the craze. It spread to the younger members of the Royal Family, and forty years later The Duke of Windsor, when Prince of Wales, echoed the refrain while the same singer was singing the same song.

There can be no doubt that the man we know as Charles Coburn was a pioneer of song-plugging, a craft which consists of persistently planting a song in one place until it takes root and spreads. He gained the name of Charles Whitton McCullum, which seems to explain his pertinacity, from his parents. He called himself Charles Lawrie when he began on the old Cockney halls, where Irish humour was welcome and Scottish humour unknown. Somebody advised him to try a crisper stage-name. He was standing, that moment, in Coborn Street, Poplar. A railway station is also named after it. He is still singing "Two Lovely Black Eyes" and he is still singing "The Man Who Broke The Bank At Monte Carlo," which reminds me of a chorister in the row behind at Collins's, who sang in a voice affected by adenoids, cold-in-the-head, pipe-on-the-tooth, frog-in-the-throat, moustache entanglements, and chronic alcoholism:

> As I strole alog der Bois de Ber-log
> Wib ab iddibeded air er
> You could 'ear der fogues deglare er
> He bub be er bidyerdaire er
> You cad 'ear derb sigh
> Ab wib deer die
> You cad see derb wig der abber eye
> Ab der bad 'oo brogue der bag ad Dod Dee Gar Doh.

Notice how complicated the chorus is compared with "Two Lovely Black Eyes," which it replaced in popular fancy. The business of teaching it to the world was very hard work. Yet it was prompted by a sudden inspiration that could not be withstood. Tom Costello tells—more dramatically than can be told in print—how Fred Gilbert pointed to the words, "Man Who Broke The Bank At Monte Carlo," on a poster in the Strand.

"There's rhythm there," said Gilbert, and began to beat his right fist against his breast, like a gorilla, as he walked.

After they had parted, he went on beating time thus to the unborn tune. He was in labour with it all day. At home his wife had a raging toothache. She suffered his obsession until nightfall, but when he beat his breast in bed, at last complained. Gilbert paced the floor in the throes of composition all that night. He worked at the same task all the next day. But when this heaven-sent song was complete, no one would have it. Many, including Albert Chevalier, had refused it before it was despairingly submitted to Coburn; and he, deciding that it was "rather too high-brow for an average music-hall audience" —so he says in the autobiography named after it—sent it back:

But no sooner had the letter and song been posted than I began to fear I had made a mistake. I went up and down the house humming the chorus, which I could not get out of my mind. I said to myself, "After all, it's only a guinea for the singing rights, apart from publication, and it certainly is a fine chorus." At last I decided that I would have it, and then began to tremble for fear somebody else had snapped it up. Early next morning I went over the water to York Corner, found Fred Gilbert's address, and went after him. Shown into his room, where he sat at a table covered with papers, I said, "Well, Fred, I've decided to have that song after all." I waited for him to say "Sorry, old chap, but I've sold it." But he didn't. He said, "All right, you can have it," and in a few seconds I became proprietor of that wonderful song.

The first time Charles Coburn plugged "The Man Who Broke The Bank At Monte Carlo" at the Oxford, he sang the chorus of the last verse *ten times*. He gagged for all he was worth in order to make the audience believe it was worth while to memorise the words. A critic declared the next day that the comedian's "salesmanship" made the audience disgusted and himself sick. "I don't wonder," was Coburn's comment. But he did not possess the name of Colin Whitton McCallum in real life for nothing. One night the manager heard him saying to himself in the glass, "It's a good song—I like it—and they'll have to like it. They've *got it* now, sir, haven't they?"

When it came to publication, the author-composer willingly accepted ten pounds for his share. Coburn handed the MS. over for "A fiver and a royalty." Then it was sung by Maggie Duggan in a Gaiety show, and the receipts went up until Coburn's share alone amounted to six hundred pounds. At the Eden, a "rough house" on the site now occupied by the Kingsway Theatre, the audience were so rowdy one night that nobody on the stage could get a hearing. Charles Coburn got the band to strike up "The Man Who Broke The Bank At Monte Carlo." After the third verse, *just to teach the ruffians a lesson*, he kept repeating the chorus until they had to stop for sheer weariness.

* * * * *

Once there was a Scottish actor who was able, despite his lack of inches, to play Svengali in the grand manner of His Majesty's.

Having a turn for writing, he amused himself by writing a couple of sketches for Lauder. They were refused. He sent them to Neil Kenyon. As they were refused again, he decided to act them himself, and he has been doing so ever since with such success that his Svengali is kept for private parties. To-day, Will Fyffe comes first in "character" on the halls. Even at a time when speed is regarded as essential to the success of every performance, when singers, dancers, musicians, jugglers, conjurers, and acrobats must all consent to restrictions of their time allowance, the delicacy of his art is so well recognised even by the strictest managements that he is freely granted all the minutes he requires for perfecting his portraits.

He was born in Dundee, where his father, who had been employed in the shipyards, was a teacher of languages at the college. After helping his grandfather, a stock-breeder, Will became an actor in a fit-up company formed by his father. Naturally his first appearance on the stage was as Little Willie in "East Lynne"—a club of Little Willies would have a very remarkable membership—and later Little Eva in "Uncle Tom's Cabin." By striking out for himself, he increased his range considerably, and at fifteen played Polonius. He learned how to be resourceful in those days. When his pistol misfired, he battered the villain's skull (in make-believe) with the butt. Some of those tours ended disastrously. In Lancashire once he was glad to act as waiter, cellarman, billiard-marker, and singer in a public-house. As soon as he "got another shop" he left. The kindly publican advised, "Think it over. Don't forget when tha changes tha mind, lad, there's still thirty bob a week ready for tha here."

It was in a touring revue, entitled "Bo-Bo," that Will Fyffe decided to be a comedian. Three years later, in the sketches he had intended for Lauder, he became a turn. On arriving in town at the Palladium, on July 18, 1921, he went straight to the top of the bill, and was included in the next Royal Variety Performance.

Every one of the Scottish worthies he has created for us is a masterpiece. We rarely see the grave ones now, although we are willing to be harrowed by his tales of sorrow because their humanity rings true. He has the power of making us forget our surroundings. Walls and roofs, proscenium arch and tabs, orchestra and audience, all vanish when he comes on the boards. The painted backcloth becomes somewhere in Scotland. Perhaps we are standing with him at a street corner in Glasgow outside, or by a cot in Perthshire, or on the Clydeside docks.

How that bridegroom of ninety-four smells of the countryside. What a real old age is his! Other actors of ancient gaffers try to walk as stiffly as possible. Will Fyffe tries to be as lively as possible—the stiffness is so natural it seems to be in his joints. This waggish old fellow, too, is not talking mere patter when he pulls the legs of Southron townsfolk. He insists that sparrows had to go down on their knees to peck his corn, it was so short, also that his potatoes were unable to see how to grow because his neighbour's onions were too strong for their eyes. Off he hobbles. Away we go to Glasgow, and here is quite another Scot who pulls his own leg. "Glasgae Belawngs Ta Me," is a lyric of "intoshtication"; its spirit is summed up in his reply to those who object to a man going home drunk—"He has to gae hame some time, hasn't he?"

In pathos Will Fyffe is equally skilled. Remember his old shepherd, telling how his sheep-dog (present on the stage) was all that was left of his kith and kin? But perhaps his most effective study is that of the village idiot, a masterly blend of laughter and tears. Every sentence he utters is packed full of meaning. When he pulls the ferret out of his bag and remarks, "Tha yoosed tae belawng to the gamekeeper," the casual tone suggests that it has been lawfully purchased, but we know at the same time that it has not. Gradually the humour softens until he comes to tell us of the widow of his best friend and the savings he has made over to her. He was not allowed to attend the funeral, because the minister was afraid he would make the people laugh.

Although he specialises in old men, his studies of middle-age are just as unctuous and mellow. Wreathed in golden whiskers like a setting sun in the tropics, he presents himself as a "gairrd" who explains why "ultimately" is a word very often used on his railway. The engine-driver cannot resist appeals for hot water from old women picnicking on the embankment; at Invershin there is always a stop of twenty-five minutes while the driver gives violin lessons to the station-master's daughter; there was a long wait between stations one day, caused by a cow on the line; later on, another stop was caused by the same cow—the train had caught it up. Contrast this with "The Gamekeeper," a Scottish cousin of Old Bill. Wearing a red wig and walrus moustache, velvet jacket, check plus-fours, and big brown boots, he describes his promotion from head poacher to head keeper.

By dressing himself up as a sailor and singing a song about sailing up the Clyde, Will Fyffe shows how good-living has added to his girth. "You pipple," he says, "must think that as I've been in America so long, I'm wearing a money belt. But this (patting his stomach) is for when I settle down and want to look out at ships approaching land. I shall rest it on the pier," whereat he indicates, in dumb show, the comfort of depositing it on a parapet.

92 CHARLES COBORN

91 WILL FYFFE

CHAPTER TWELVE

Very Tragical Mirth

THAT fiction of a lover's broken heart beneath the motley may not be strictly related to fact. Even so, although the ache of unrequited passion rarely, if ever, twists the face under the comic make-up, there is often a wince from other kinds of pain. I laughed for an hour or more one Boxing Day at Douglas Wakefield's fretfulness as the Robber, pestered by the Babes while taking them to be murdered in the Wood. He was too pained to speak. The next day I found he had taken to his bed, not being able to speak, on the stage or off.

Private miseries seem to add to a comedian's public mirth. Mark Sheridan, in his gloomiest years, came on the boards the merriest soul alive with his Dick Swiveller swagger. In tilted, decayed topper, in gangrened frock-coat, in trousers that shrank as tights to his thighs and swelled below the knees into flapping bell-bottoms, he strutted up and down, swinging his cane, and banging the stage with it to add conviction to every "here" in "Here We Are Again." That was his War song which spread to every front. In happier times his favourite songs had been seaside ones, sung on the other kind of front. The seaside aroused in him such delight that he seemed lost in contemplation of the view he loved of waves and sands—on the backcloth. You might imagine he had forgotten his audience until after he had gone round with the hat to the painted holiday-makers. Then he remembered to amuse us by pointing out the girl in a bathing costume as Maud Allan—"So much on she's nearly suffocated, poor girl!"

There were other seaside songs at that time but none fit to rank with Mark Sheridan's. He not only expressed the ecstasy of Cockneys on holiday, but he added to it. Esplanades rang with his choruses. Everybody *did* like to be beside the seaside. If Noel Coward had written at that time his lyric about wishing you were dead on finding sand in your bed, he would have been cheered as a nonsensical humorist instead of a satirist: as a matter of fact, Dan Leno's seaside song, "Never More," did gain that effect with much the same sentiments. "Here We Are Again" was always Mark Sheridan's spirit on the stage: and the moral was that everybody was always glad to be there again no matter where the "here" might be—"prom.," trench, the Strand, or home after the War.

Yet that ancient cry he had borrowed from Joey, the clown, points
to his tragedy. It occurred at the one place above all others on earth
where he had expected to find happiness—because he had found it
there long before he arrived in London at the Standard, Pimlico
(where the Victoria Palace now stands), in the early 'nineties. That
place was Glasgow. Since it had been the first to recognise his powers,
he went there hopefully for the Christmas season of 1917. But
Scottish audiences are not only quick to reward talent; they are also
quick to note its decay and there can be little doubt that Mark Sheridan
was losing grip. He became the victim of comedian's misanthropy.
He suffered from it so severely that because he had heard jeers—and
for no other known reason—he went out one bleak morning into a
deserted park and there shot himself.

*   *   *   *   *

Of all the sad figures of very tragical mirth who flit before the
mind's eye, none makes our heart ache more than George Formby.
Here is no tale of misspent opportunities or expended fortunes. He
was nothing more romantic, nothing less heroic, than the father of a
family, struggling against time to provide for his wife and children.
Time was short. Soon after he had come to London from the provinces, where his career began in 1899, he found that what he had
taken to be a troublesome cough was sentence of death. Perhaps he
could have survived it if he had gone to live in the country at once,
but he had discovered, in that cough, the means to keep people
laughing.

"Coughing better to-night, George," he would say to the conductor, "Coughing summat champion."

John Willie from Lancashire, the character he created on the halls,
was made to fit that cough. He was full of a desire to justify himself
to the audiences who laughed at his stupidity. He was only "Standing
at the corner of the street," when the recruiting sergeant found him;
and it was not his fault that he got lost in Madame Tussaud's. His
songs all had this self-explanatory tone of a timid, diffident soul who
wanted to put himself right with the world. He boasted about
having met Florrie Forde, and sang, "I'm Such A Hit With The
Girls," "One Of The Boys," and "Playing The Game In The West."
He dearly wanted to brag ("Since I Parted My Hair In The Middle,"
was another example), so that when he had to stop to cough the
effect was comical.

The "trick" never failed to excite outbursts of laughter. The
audience was still laughing when he was standing in the wings,
gasping for breath, before staggering back painfully to his dressing-
room. The first night of the revue, "Razzle-Dazzle," at Drury Lane,

From a song-front by courtesy of Messrs. B. Feldman & Co.

in the June of 1916, was for him a terrible ordeal. The doctor had warned him not to go on. George Formby had to, though death might be his partner. The secret was well kept, he attempted his mock acrobatic feat of picking up a handkerchief, with such difficulty that the feat had never before seemed so amusing, and he was helped back to a couch where his wife lay by his side, pressing herself against his side to bring ease to his wasted lungs. He kept going just long enough before his death to tide his family over until George Formby Junior, now a smart light comedian, idolised in the North, should shoulder the responsibilities he had borne with such unromantic heroism.

★   ★   ★   ★   ★

In such affection is all that belonged to the old music-hall held now, that we forget there was ever a revulsion of feeling against it. This change was directed chiefly against the red-nosed comedian—"the type," he was called, "which was once the staple commodity of the music-halls, the idiotically garbed, hideously made-up article whose only claim to attention was that it was totally unlike anything ever seen outside a lunatic asylum, that it never once 'held the mirror up to nature,' and that it was, in the main, vulgar without being funny." Sentiments of that kind, filling many minds, led to the deaths of several favourites, among them T. E. Dunville.

The new order of things came in when the theatres of variety, which replaced the old halls, took over the task, from the dying Nigger Minstrels, of entertaining the guileless and the young. Half-term holiday audiences of mothers, aunts, school-ma'ams, curates and children were being catered for at the expense of labourers and wage-earners who needed boisterous enjoyment. In the midst of edifying programmes of drawing-room ballads and humour in evening dress, the "comic" felt as embarrassed as a navvy at a Kensington At Home. "Honest vulgarity" was strictly banned. In its place we eventually had dishonest vulgarity, references to unspeakable things in jests that seemed simple to nobody except those who lived too comfortably cut off from unpleasant realities to realise that if you try to curb the love of laughter in one way it will break out in another.

For some years we were deprived of red-nosed funny men. Every imaginable kind of attraction was billed except them. We saw famous actor-managers as top-liners, we had the Russian Ballet; we had lawn-tennis champions, races by fox-terrier champions, madrigal-singing undergraduates and cowboys from the Wembley Rodeo. A demonstration of television came next, and finally all the leading theatres of variety in town gave up "variety" altogether and presented talking-films—permanently or temporarily—instead. The music-halls had been too weakened by the policy of relying on outside interests to oppose the popularity of the films.

This period in the history of the halls must be recalled before we can understand the depths of despair which ended the lives of funny men in tragedy. Among them was T. E. Dunville, the "eccentric" who used to sing:

> A little boy,
> A pair of skates,
> Broken ice,
> Heaven's gates.

In his book, *The Autobiography of an Eccentric Comedian*, he says his name was taken from a whisky bottle. To explain his first hankering for the stage, he recalls Coventry Fair:

There I saw various shows, including a performance of Pepper's Ghost, the effect of which upon me was such that I fainted directly I got home! Anyhow, from that time I began to practise high-kicking.

When apprenticed to a silk merchant, he performed acrobatic feats in the counting-house until shifted to the store-department. Next he set out for London with two other youths as a nigger minstrel troupe called "The Three Spires" after the Three Spires of Coventry. Unfortunately they wore their Sunday clothes, so that at the public-houses at Dunchurch, where they went round with the hat among men not so well dressed as themselves, they usually had to "stand drinks all round in order to obtain an appreciative audience." They travelled as far as Weedon and then returned home to Coventry penniless.

At sixteen he and a friend did contrive to appear on a stage. They were allowed to appear in a touring pantomime at Barnsley. They were to begin by walking backwards and forwards, kicking over each other's heads, and end by falling from a table backwards, each into a barrel. At the first performance, Dunville kicked his partner on the ear until his face "grew as red with pain and boiling indignation as were the faces of the entire audience through the roars of laughter which ensued." The finale was worse. The apple barrels they were using were so much taller than those they had used at rehearsals, that the young acrobats sank out of sight and became so firmly stuck that they could not move hand or foot. Stage hands had to roll them off, barrels and all. The manager was pleased with them. All that he desired was that they should repeat those blunders and daub a little red paint on the end of their noses.

One of the members of the company, turning actor-manager, engaged them to play a pair of keepers in a lunatic asylum for a comic

opera called "Abou." Later they went to America to appear at
Manhattan Beach in an open-air display called "The Fall Of Pompeii,"
as statues who amazed the priests by leaving their pedestals for an
acrobatic dance. On returning to England they were a pair of bailiffs
in "The Babes In The Wood" at Leicester, at the time little Vesta
Tilley represented the Clerk of the Weather. Engagements were so
regular that Dunville became a solo turn. It was a disillusioning
experience at first:

There was real hard work attached to one's profession then, harder work,
by a long way, than there is to-day even when one has to play four halls a
night. As a rule one turned up on the Monday morning to ask if there was
an opening, and as likely as not, the proprietor of the public-house would
say, "Cut in! Let us see what you can do." And then and there one would
open one's little handbag, make-up with the aid of such properties as one had,
and do a comic song and dance upon the sanded floor of the taproom for
the benefit, very often, of no more than a couple of workmen who might
happen to be there at the moment. If the publican and these worthies approved,
one perhaps obtained an engagement for the week, which meant being ready
to give a song at constant intervals throughout the day, as often as there was
anyone in the bar. It was only in the evening that a more ordered show was
given in the special room set aside for that purpose, and as a rule two, or at
the outside three, artists had to provide a programme which was made to
extend over the entire evening till closing time.
Oh, I can almost shed tears when I think of those old days! One's repertoire
of half-a-dozen songs or so was gone through again and again during the day,
but must be repeated in its entirety during the evening, although to many of
those present much of one's "business" might be stale. The air thick with
the fumes of shag-laden pipes, the temperature about 80°, the concentrated
reek of beer, the raucous calls for fresh supplies, the rattle of pint pots in
applause, the oaths and shouts of derision if one failed to please, have left an
impression on my mind that I shall carry with me to my grave!

One Monday in the March of 1889, as "extra turn" for a farmer's
matinée at the Victoria Music Hall, Bolton, Dunville's luck changed.
That autumn he opened in London at the Middlesex in Drury Lane,
Gatti's-Under-The-Arches at Charing Cross, and the Foresters. He
remained in London for months at a stretch, particularly at the
Trocadero where his engagements lasted for four or five months.
Apart from one sad night when he tried to alter his make-up, he
remained a firm favourite until the change in music-hall fashions that
drove him to his death.
He was always idiotically garbed and hideously made-up; and he
loved to sing such scraps of nonsense as "Dinky-Doo" and "Bunk-A-
Doodle-I-Do" and "Pop, Pop, Popperty-Pop." Off the stage he
had a solemnity rather like that of Buster Keaton, the hero of many
comic silent films. On the stage, Dunville still had a mournful look,

and his angular gestures suggested an underfed curate. These were in contrast to his clownish clothes, his huge white cuffs and spreading Eton collars, his flapping trousers, and his bizarre taste in hats.

In 1890 you might have heard him sing an "evening-dress burlesque song," but he soon stuck to eccentricity for good. He was a favourite for years, steadily increasing in popularity until the great change occurred and then it was too late to return to evening dress. He took the lack of encouragement to heart, unaware that the falling-off was not peculiar to himself; his funds were running short, but he was not penniless. One day in 1924 he went to a favourite resort of players and scribblers in Leicester Square. Somebody, who might have been equally hard hit by the turn of events, said, "Here's the fallen star." Dunville walked out. For some days he was missing. Then his body was found in "Suicide's Lock," near Reading.

★ ★ ★ ★ ★

Is there any country in the whole of the wide, wide world where "Daisy Bell" has not been heard? It is as popular in America as in Great Britain, and it has spread right across Europe. I remember visiting a cabaret in Budapest and being saluted, the moment my nationality was known, with this song. A fascinating visitor from a place equally remote sang "Daisee, Daisee, geeve mee y'r answer trooo," the first evening she arrived in London. Yet over twenty years have passed since Katie Lawrence, who made it popular in this country, died. Although not a reigning beauty of the halls, she had a look of quick, humorous intelligence which was very taking even when she wore a trilby hat and starched collar in mockery of masculine fashions. Are any of her other songs remembered? "Rosey-Posey" is sometimes hummed by old fogies—but they are usually very old fogies. She also had a seaside song, called, "She Looked A Perfect Lady," and a woeful tale of love, called "Mary Jane," that are worth reviving. There are probably quite a number of others we should be glad to hear—but none other with the glamorous quality of "The songs that never die."

In the hey-day of "Daisy Bell" Katie Lawrence could well afford a carriage. She was much sought after and everybody was eager to receive invitations to visit her at Bell House, hard by the Zoo, in Regent's Park Road. She married George Fuller, who was interested in racing ponies. But their money vanished, and their next home, though not far away, was a far less opulent affair in Camden Town. There the husband died of cancer, and Katie Lawrence's circumstances became more and more desperate. Yet she still possessed much of her old charm and soon had suitors. She became engaged to be married at a time when managers seemed to have forgotten her.

Fortunately her old friends of the boards had not. Marie Lloyd, coming to the rescue, sent her clothes for her trousseau. But Katie Lawrence's troubles were not over. She died in poverty.

★　★　★　★　★

We still witness outbreaks of the "banjo mania" which has disturbed the world's peace at odd intervals since 1840. During a particularly virulent outbreak in Durban, a musician was busily engaged spreading the fever. About the time he came to a tragic end, one of his pupils, a young engine-fitter on the Government railways, began to play in public. That was the start of Franco Piper's career. I marvelled at his circle of spinning banjoes as a child, and I marvelled still on his return to the halls as a "veteran." Although he was a novelty to the new generation, very few engagements followed. Enforced idleness away from the boards drove him to suicide. One May night in 1933 he was found in his car on a by-road leading to the Sussex Downs, a few miles from Steyning. He had shot himself with a revolver.

There was also Tom D. Newell, a popular Dame. While the Widow Twankey of a Liverpool pantomime in 1928, he heard a radio message between the acts, calling him to Llandudno, where his son was dying after a motor accident. Tom Newell stayed to the fall of the curtain, and drove through the night, but he arrived too late. Seven years later, near the Whoop Hall Inn at Kirkby Lonsdale, Westmoreland, he was shot through the heart from his own gun, while pigeon-shooting.

In the August of 1935, John Tilley—whose real name was Thomson —died after a career as a comedian that lasted three years. While singing in a rest camp during the War, he was advised by Jack Tilley of the Alhambra, to go on the stage. Thomson inherited a fortune of £7000 and lost it, sold moth-proof bags, worked in a bank and a cold storage plant, sold paint, and then joined the advertising staff of a newspaper. Next, through meeting the manager who was turning a cinema into the Windmill Variety Theatre, he gave a trial turn at an audition which installed him as comedian of the show. He married an attendant at the theatre and prospered so well that he was engaged as the leading actor of a West End play. But he was a sick man. He lived only long enough to win back nearly as much as the fortune he had lost.

96, 97 TWO MUSIC-HALL TURNS—ONE THE FATHER OF A FILM STAR

100 BILLY BENNETT

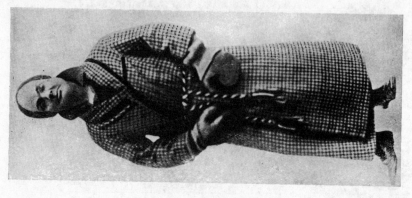

99 HARRY WELDON

98 CHARLIE CHAPLIN

CHAPTER THIRTEEN

Mumming Birds

"SCENE—The Frivolity Music Hall," says the programme. The "tabs" part, and there is its stage, flanked by boxes. Into one comes "The Inebriated Swell," known to us as "the drunk," and into the other the grey-haired dignified father of a fat boy who wears an Eton suit and carries a pea-shooter as well as greengrocery and buns. Odd performers who appear before the landscape on the miniature blackcloth, have to suffer criticism of a particularly severe nature, for what blow could pen or typewriter deliver compared with the impact of such very large buns? While the boy rids himself of rations enough for a school in this manner, the "drunk" pulls the number of the turn from its frame and calls for another bottle. A tramp juggler wanders on, asks the whereabouts of the elephants he has to "follow," and wanders off. A conjurer wishes to deceive the eye, but all his tricks are spoiled; two strong men try a feat of balance until one has his trousers pulled off by "the drunk" and has to leave his partner in mid-air; meanwhile, the tramp juggler is still looking for the elephants, and the boy is still throwing buns at every turn except the *serio comic* with calves like Victorian table legs.

That, roughly, was "Mumming Birds," the sketch that made Fred Karno known the world over as an expert of knockabout humour. At his birth, at Exeter in 1866, his surname was Westcott, and so it remained while he learned grim lessons as a child-worker at a Nottingham loom. He earned enough money as a plumber's boy at a prison to buy his training as a gymnast, and so became one of the Karno Trio. Talks with the convicts (so he says) helped him when he devised "Jail Birds," which he boosted by driving his company to the stage-doors of music-halls in a "Black Maria" he had bought second-hand.

Thus Fred Karno bestowed on the music-hall the gift of inconsequential nonsense. One of his players, Charles Chaplin, took that gift to the films when he left the company on a tour through America and went to Hollywood. Other members of "Karno's Komics" left to develop the idea on their own. One was Fred Kitchen, who was the son of a popular clown and had been on the stage since childhood.

Q

Another was Harry Weldon, who began life as a florist. In Fred
Karno's football sketch he was the goalkeeper who leaned dolefully
against a post, trying vainly to fold his arms, and then (because they
would slip through one another) trying to put his hands in his pockets,
only to find his shorts had no pockets. "Are we alone?" asked
Chaplin, the villain of the piece. "No," said Weldon. "Who's
here?" asked Chaplin. "Me," said Weldon.

Each Karno graduate developed a special style of his training.
Chaplin reflected the pathos of fooling, and Kitchen its cheerful side.
With "Stiffy The Goalkeeper," his first rôle after leaving the "Komics,"
Harry Weldon began to specialise in anti-heroics. No romantic type,
after that, was safe from his jesting. As the great pugilist, he added
to his manager's challenge to all-comers of "Will any gentleman?"
the plea, "Will any lady?" As the toreador, he boasted how he forced
the bull to kiss him by making a noise like a cow. As the prison
warder, he knitted a pair of socks for a convict who wanted to go to
a fancy-dress ball. When an attempt was made to break out of jail,
he told the desperate characters to sit down, and brushed their hair
lest they should give the prison a bad name. Some minutes later they
returned because it was raining. "Oh well," said the warder, "you
can't mess the prison about. Either you stay in or you go out; one
thing or the other. There's other people wanting to come in besides
you."

In this way he cracked the jest of reversing reality. He made topsy-
turveydom strictly logical. His large, ponderously reflective face
helped, and also his quavering voice. His trick of long-drawn-out
sibilants was imitated everywhere. There was a time when his catch-
phrase of "'s no use" echoed in every street. In his hey-day, shortly
after the War, there was no other comedian so certain to make
audiences laugh. But three or four years before his death in 1930,
he felt the strain that overwhelms so many comedians in middle-age.
The weariness of a life without a rest from mirth embittered him as
it had embittered so many besides.

*   *   *   *   *

Although never a member of "The Karno Combination," Charles
Austin expresses their spirit in "Parker, P.C." Which Parker gave
his name to be a label for persons of inordinate curiosity may not be
discovered, but we can record how it has gained another meaning.
It began the day Charles Austin noticed a disused police-station with
a "To Let" notice in the window.

"Suppose," he thought, "they discharged a constable at the new
place. Suppose he set up shop on his own account in the old place.

Suppose he cut prices, with crimes and offences to suit every purse." That was how Parker, P.C. was born.

Since then his character has been revealed in a variety of circumstances. What he symbolises is the awkwardness of "the layman," that is to say, of the human being who tries to carry out the duties of a profession for which he is not qualified either by nature or art. Parker never understands the station in life to which it has pleased Charles Austin to call him. In the post-office he held up a sheet of postage stamps to his customer, pointed to the middle one, and asked whether that was the one he would like to buy. Even in a scene of the British Empire Exhibition at Wembley he could not behave normally; he was a "layman" even at holiday-making.

Later he went "on the pictures," where he represented blushing inexperience convinced of latent talent. Nervousness made him very talkative, and given to gigglings and a cough, but he overcame this. Full of assurance, he seized the chance to crank the camera, only to find at the end of the scene that he had been holding it the wrong way round. And later he showed how even the winner of the Irish Sweepstake can be a failure. In the very act of buying the ticket, he leaves it in the jacket which he pawns to obtain the purchase price. Before the draw he has promised half his winnings to the bookie and the other half to the village constable for police protection. All he gains from the victory of the horse he has drawn is the pleasure of smoking two cigars at once.

Austin is a Londoner. He was a clerk in a lawyer's office before he became, at English's Sebright Music Hall, in 1896, one of two "Stage Struck Waifs."

* * * * *

Once upon a time "almost a gentleman" could be said with a patronising and condescending air. Now it can only be uttered in a tone of admiration. Billy Bennett, typifying some significant quality of his generation, has effected the change. The phrase no longer conjures up a picture of honest worth and perfectly good manners apart from "sporting" a tie. Instead, there is hair with a fringe curled by the curlers, moustache lamentably unclipped, dress-suit with a hiatus, an item of feminine harness in place of fob, and brown boots. Clothes make not only the man but the "almost" in gentleman. The poem he is about to recite is by the greatest of living authors. "And when I finished writing it," he goes on to say . . . there is no dissentient voice.

Which is the best of Billy Bennett's almost poetical works may be decided by the literary and debating societies of the future. What we may be sure of now, however, is that "The Sailor's Farewell To His Horse" is the most characteristic.

> The little sardines had gone into their tins
> And pulled down the lid for the night,

is as soothing as

> I saw lots of water on top of the waves
> And I found a lot more underneath

is agitating. We have never discovered what became of the sailor's horse. Perhaps he was the one swallowed by the bearded man who looked as though he had "eaten a horse and left the tail hanging out of his mouth."

The scene changes, and Billy Bennett wears a canvas suit topped by a sun helmet that is a walking tent. It is so hot on that stretch of the road to Mandalay which he trudges, that he is glad to drink out of a hot-water bottle while he tells his tale of soldiers' tongues hanging out and dragging along the sands until the natives think that an English furnishing establishment has been laying a carpet on the desert.

★　★　★　★　★

Since she also is expert in unrelated nonsense, Nellie Wallace may be brought into this class. Just to be let loose on the stage gives her so much joy that she performs an *entrechat* in each corner. She is free from the indelicacy of the ballerina. Instead of frills and laces, she exposes what seems to be an expanse of lurid wallpaper. "It's excitement—all excitement," she cries. "If you're fond of anything *tasty*, what price me?" She performs all the tricks of feminine allure in a skin-tight evening gown that puts her at a disadvantage when she drops her fan and has to lie full length, because she cannot bend, to pick it up. "Strange," she exclaims, looking at the clock, "he promised to be here at 9.30. It is now twelve o'clock." With that she looks towards us to excite our sympathy with a despairing sniff over protruding teeth and a heart-rending squint.

She was born at Glasgow, during a lecture tour given by her father, with her mother as pianist. Her first appearance on the halls was as a child clog dancer, before she became one of the Three Sisters Wallace. She acted in theatres with her parents until her success as a comedian while playing Little Willie's death scene in "East Lynne" sent her back to the boards as a single turn.

101 NELLIE WALLACE

From a photograph by Cecil Beaton

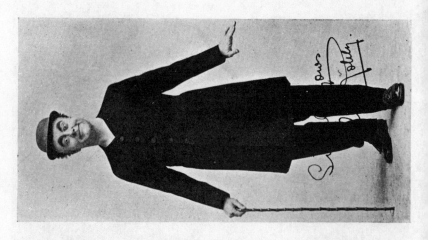

CHAPTER FOURTEEN

George Robey—Harry Tate— Billy Merson

As Shakespeare's Falstaff on the stage, as Cervantes' Sancho Panza on the screen, and as Joey in a harlequinade, George Robey has so often transformed himself in recent years that we can never be sure what he will be doing next. So far he has never tackled a tragic part in all seriousness, but he has been contemplating Shylock. Why not? He is well equipped for the task. Good fairies showered into his cradle the gifts of emphatic speech, forthright gesture, significant pose and arresting glance as though intending him for the great tragedian of his generation. And yet the fairy of mischief won. By ordaining that he should begin his career as assistant to a mesmerist, she caused him to daub red on his nose instead of the left breast of his shirt. You may still infer from his acting that a music-hall comedian may be a tragedian who has overtrained. His stern decrees, such as, "I shall not speak again. If one of you has to go, you will all go," are uttered with a serenity that only the affability of his eyes, under jet eyebrows formed like the arches of vanished Waterloo Bridge, could check.

Oddly contrasted surroundings influenced his budding genius. He was born on September 20, 1869, at Herne Hill, London, but spent some part of his childhood near Birkenhead. When the London suburbs were about to have a service of horse-drawn trams, his father was the engineer who supervised the laying of the lines in "Camberwell sarf-east." The next removal was to Dresden, where George Robey prepared to become a doctor of science. Before that could happen the family returned to England. He was a Cambridge undergraduate for a time; next an engineer in Birmingham, which owes its tramway system to him (among others). On the mandoline he played duets with a friend on the guitar, at charity concerts; in an emergency he made his first attempt at singing in public. Back in London he earned fees as an entertainer at private parties. The next step was an introduction to Kennedy, the mesmerist, at the music-hall of the Aquarium (opposite Westminster Abbey on the site where the Central Hall now stands). At his own suggestion Robey was engaged as his assistant. There is no truth, however, in the persistent legend that he had pins stuck in him. What actually happened he has himself described :

At a certain point in the programme the mesmerist glared at me, projected his arms, and executed a few rapid passes. Like a person in a dream I rose. My face slipped, my eyes grew vacant. Then, apparently obeying his command, I groped my way up to the stage amid a general hush that could be felt. The other "subjects" on the stage—old hands at the game—looked on with interest. I walked up to the performer, closed my eyes, and waited. He began to make "passes" over me. "Don't forget," I whispered to him through lips almost closed like a ventriloquist's, "I am a comic singer!" I heard him breathe deeply. Then he exclaimed in a loud voice. "Young man, you are now under my power. You will do whatever I tell you. *You are a comic singer.*"

All went well at the start. Everybody laughed when he sang "A Little Peach In An Orchard Grew," until a jealous "subject" kicked him over the footlights into the stalls. Robey stood up, caught the mesmeric eye, and went on with his song. He was mesmerised nightly without hope of payment until offered a place in a trial matinée at the Oxford, which led to the signing of a year's contract. In 1891, when that happened, he already possessed the famous eyebrows though dressed as a "toff" in brown bowler, high collar, huge pale-blue cravat, yellow waistcoat, and vermilion jacket. It was for "The Simple Pimple," another of his earliest songs, that he dressed himself as a parson, though he did not find his clerical self right away. There was a simper on his face, and he had a high, bald forehead, which a long lock of hair, rooted just above one ear, tried vainly to cover. That was the origin of the round-faced, impudent-eyed *decolleté* curate, wearing a very flat hat and swishing a vertebrate cane, we see in imagination whenever we hear the words, "Prime Minister Of Mirth." This character is not merely George Robey's greatest creation : as far as the general public is concerned, he *is* George Robey—far more than the person who answers to this name in private life.

Yet he has acted scores of other characters. You may remember him as Oliver Cromwell, giving the order, "Take away that bauble —take it away and see how much you can get on it." You have certainly seen him as the bland, self-satisfied professor of music from Germany, shaking a collar of sleigh bells, tinkling a triangle, banging a drum, and carefully avoiding more difficult instruments in the formidable array set on the stage to proclaim his virtuosity. Then there is Sir Walter Raleigh, with his story of being on the shore waiting to receive Columbus when he discovered America; also the auctioneer, with his offer to the woman who wants a hen that would eat sawdust and lay firewood, of a love-bird which "eats feathers and lays down." At one time he transformed himself into Cupid and at another into Shakespeare. All these changes occurred while he was still content to act on the halls.

Since he became talked about from the very start of his career, George Robey has been a public character for nearly fifty years. His zenith *seemed* to have been reached during the long run, lasting well over a year, of "The Bing Boys Are Here" at the Alhambra during the War. As village boys looking for life in London, he (the devilish one) and Alfred Lester (the mournful, misgiving one), were let loose in a night club where chorus girls sat on their knees, drank their champagne and went off without granting them a look or a word. Lucifer Bing's emotions were such that while a bishop and a general published protests in the Press, audiences shouted with laughter night after night. After raising a quarter of a million for war charities by organising concerts and holding auctions on the stage, he joined the Motor Transport Volunteers. At the end of the War, the O.B.E. was conferred upon him.

For a while he tried his hand at films. Next he went into management with the revue, "Bits And Pieces," which he took on tour in the provinces, South Africa and Canada, in between seasons in the West End. We thought he was settling down into the usual groove of successful comedians, before he took us by surprise as Sancho Panza to the Don Quixote of Chaliapine on the films. But this was nothing compared to the news, proclaimed by newsboys' bills all over London, of his intention to play Falstaff in "Henry IV. Part I." Great expectations filled His Majesty's Theatre in the spring of 1935, and he lived up to them. Only pedants noted what difficulties he had with the text. Everybody else applauded his happy touches of impudence. He came down to the footlights to say to the audience, "I am accursed," in his music-hall manner, and he followed up an Elizabethan impropriety with a look in his "desist from mirth" manner.

★   ★   ★   ★   ★

What *Alice in Wonderland* is to nursery or study, Harry Tate's sketches are to the stage. As the one loses its magic when acted, so the others are not meant for cold print. Yet Lewis Carroll and Tate are alike in one essential thing. While unlike life as we know it,' they are so consistent, so logical according to their own laws of cause and effect, that we soon lose ourselves in the illusion that their worlds exist. After the village idiot in "Fishing" has explained that he is casting snuff on the waters so that "when the fish comes up to sneeze I hits them on the head with this (*shows stick*)," we are no more surprised at the size, richness and variety of his catch than at the behaviour of the White Rabbit or the White Knight.

Harry Tate was not ever thus—nor is he now, for as a film actor he has discarded the famous moustache which revolved half-way and back again like a propeller that is being cranked up (or so it seems to a mind ignorant of engines). "Scotland," he states, was the place where he was born on July 4, 1872. His name was Ronald Macdonald Hutchinson, and as such he was employed by Henry Tate and Sons, sugar refiners. At smoking concerts he developed his powers of entertainment, especially as a mimic, and it was as Harry Tate, mimic, that he gained a trial hearing at the Oxford on April 13, 1895. His earliest material consisted of two "vehicles" for his imitations, called "Number Seven," and "A Ward In Chancery," as well as the songs "The Cabbie's Lament" and "How's Your Father?" Then began that association with Wal Pink, also a singer of comic songs at the outset, which produced the richest cream of music-hall nonsense.

Perhaps it was because Wal Pink's hobbies were motoring and fishing that the idea of their sporting sketches was born. Motoring in those days was a very uncertain method of getting from one place to another, and fishing has long been proverbial for the contrasts it affords between expectation and realisation, as well as between realisation and retrospection. Everybody in the length and breadth of the land from King Edward on his throne to small boys with catapult and stone, saw the joke of "Motoring." It was the favourite jest of royalty, from private parties at Marlborough House to the first Royal Variety Performance at the Palace in 1912, when Harry Tate gained his title of "The man who made the Queen laugh."

His company consisted of players as unique as their parts, queer-looking, queer-sounding "boys," and also Kennedy with his air of great civility and red nose. Where Harry Tate found his boys was a mystery; they were all quite different and all equally unlike real life. There was his "son" who wore a topper while sitting in the back of the car and shouting "Good-bye-eee" more and more energetically when it refused to move. The way he said "Pa Pa" left us, in itself, helpless with laughter, and we were in pain when, after solemnly declaring that the car would not go because the wheels were not round, he explained to his exasperated parent at the end of their debate that what he had meant was that they were not going round. "Motoring" was a classic of nonsense, and so was "Fishing" with its scene of a peaceful Thames backwater, where bottles are set up in rows before the incomplete angler rouses the sleeper in a punt by throwing loaves upon the water. Mr. Tate thinks there are tons

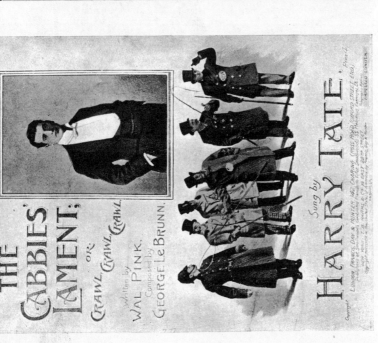

104, 105 HARRY TATE—FROM SONG-FRONT AND PHOTOGRAPH

THE LAST GOOD-BYE.

This Song may be Sung in public without fee or licence
except at Music Halls and Theatres.
Theatrical permissions may be obtained of the Publishers.

CHORUS.

'Tis the last good-bye, you must take your place in the line,
Go and do your duty, Jack, I'll do mine.
I'll work for the Children as a Soldier's wife should do,
And while their father is fighting the foe,
I'll be Mother and Father too.

WRITTEN AND
COMPOSED BY
MURRAY
AND LEIGH,

Sung with the Greatest Possible Success by

MISS FLORRIE FORDE.

Copyright.

Price 4/-

HOPWOOD & CREW LTD
LATE HOWARD & CO. Music Publishers and Printers, 25, GREAT MARLBOROUGH ST. LONDON, W.
NEW YORK: W. B. GRAY & CO. 16, WEST 27TH STREET.
Copyright MDCCCC, in the United States of America, by Hopwood & Crew. Ltd

of fish about. His boatman says, "Not quite so much." Mr. Tate
is surprised. "Then how," he says, "d'you account for that?" The
boatman answers, "They took about seven tons out last week."

Why was all that fuss made about "expressionism" on the stage?
Far from being a novelty made in Germany, it had been Harry Tate's
stock-in-trade for years. Consider "Golfing" as an example. The
scene is not the links as seen by ourselves but as distorted by the hero's
"liver." At first the green, the club-house, the snoozing doyen and
the peaceful sea are fairly ordinary, but no sooner has the new member
remembered that the entrance fee cost him twenty guineas than
everything, animate or inanimate, becomes malignant. Caged
geraniums crash upon his head directly he sets foot on the verandah,
the awakened doyen nags him, the caddie refuses to speak or move,
the clubs are shaped like saucepans or things for cleaning drains, a
large swirl of tissue paper hovers ever before his eyes, and a bunker
collapses to the sound of human death-cries. At last he can stand
the caddie no longer. Each vents his anger on the other's head-gear,
but while the new member's is a bowler the boy's is a tam-o-shanter.
Even if you are no golfer, you will recognise all this as fate's usual
ambush for disgruntled man.

Though humour is a matter for very diverse opinions, Harry Tate
is able, at one and the same time, to satisfy both those who like it
subtle and those who like it plain. "Selling A Car" is an admirable
example of his gift. There is nothing in the scene that a child could
fail to understand, and yet the acutest observer must delight in nonsense that so cleverly hits off the nonsense of real life. Take, for
instance, the dialogue between Harry Tate and his "son's" college
chum. "Haven't I met you before?" asks the boy. He mentions a
certain staircase King Charles slept on, the landing at the top, the
room with three windows that were reduced to two, the windmill,
the stream that ran downhill and the pillar box at the bottom. Then
the son takes a hand and describes the lighthouse, adding the story
of how it was built and how unavailing it was. On the verge of
losing his temper, Harry Tate demands of the chum, "What is it
you want anyway?" and the boy replies, "Well, how are you?"
. . . . If your mind were thus distracted in the midst of an attempt to
sell a car, it would seem to you also that directly a purchaser arrived,
the wheels were flying off, the bottom dropping out and the cover
falling in.

During the War, Harry Tate was in revues, "Business As Usual,"
"Push And Go," and "Joyland," at the London Hippodrome. One
of his scenes in these was an office where the self-important business
man owned a lump of sugar bound with string, that was dipped in
his tea and returned to the safe. He was a stickler for "system" so

that when an office boy was being engaged, Harry Tate went out of the office and gazed at him through secret windows. New inventions were his chief concern. There was a mouse-trap with the "No thoroughfare" sign to direct the captive to a cupboard empty enough to break its heart, and so lead it on to sound the gong intended to rouse the household. There was an indicator rifle with an arrow to point out the number of rabbits required, or be kept at zero when the sportsman wanted hares. There was a sandbagging chair which Harry Tate sank into when exhausted.

After the War, he acted "Peacehaven." With a sickle in one hand and a turf-cutter in the other, he comes down to his country home to enjoy peace and quiet. Flinging down his instruments he shouts, "Bought two more of these," to a gardener already at his wit's end to know how to use a scythe on a perfectly kept lawn. With his shears Harry Tate clips several budding branches. The gardener, trying to keep him occupied in learning the names of plants, draws particular attention to a german sausage with a sprig of parsley growing out of one end.

"That's *sarve*. Took me two years to grow that," says the gardener with pride.

"Oh, is it?" says his employer, who forthwith—plying the shears in the manner of a man performing the most delicate of operations— snaps it in two.

★　★　★　★　★

The mournful little man, full of the fun of baffled yearnings for romance, who tried to be a pirate skipper or Spanish serenader, was one of the darlings of the old halls before they changed. Everybody knew Billy Merson and everybody sang "Yacki-Hicki-Doola" and "The Spaniard That Blighted My Life." They were outstanding examples of the Edwardian mockeries of Mid-Victorian glamours. There were other comedians who appeared regularly in trappings that had formerly belonged to heroes and villains much admired in melodrama and novelettes. But Billy Merson went straight to the top of their class. It was not to be wondered at. Making a start by winning a circus competition for the best display of amateur gym-nastics, he had been through the mill most thoroughly. In his book, *Fixing the Stoof Oop*, he describes the concerts of himself and a partner in small halls as SNAKELLA AND TRAVELLA, Great Acrobatic Speciality. That was how William Henry Thompson, as he had been known until then, came to play the Old Man of the Sea in a Nuneaton pantomime at the Christmas of 1901. When the staircase act of Snakella and Travella changed into the comedy duo of Keith and Merson, the partners tossed a coin to decide which name belonged to which. Billy, as the loser, took the hind part of the title.

If he kept all his old wigs in a glass case they would set forth the history of the halls most significantly. At the start he wore his false hair in the Dan Leno fashion with a broad parting in the middle. As soon as he became a single turn he went to a theatrical store in Manchester which had a basketful of wigs, and picked out, simply because it was the right size, that famous auburn one, "with a bald patch at the back of the head and two coy curls across the top of the high forehead." While wearing that in a pantomime, he first sang about Alphonso Spagoni, the toreador—"The Spaniard That Blighted My Life."

Next came his career in Albert De Courville's revues at the London Hippodrome, when he brought Hamlet up-to-date with the aid of typewriter and film, and burlesqued Somerset Maugham's melo-dramatic "Land of Promise" in a log-cabin scene which echoed to his cry of, "What a hell of a night for a honeymoon." When De Courville asked him to "tone down" his wig, he willingly "weakened" his make-up and discarded the faithful copy of his original wig. The next change occurred in "Rose Marie" at Drury Lane, when he laid wigs aside altogether. On his return to variety at the Coliseum he continued to wear his own hair and clothes that fitted him. Once more, as though for the last time, he sang the ballads whose titles had become professional phrases, of the days when he used to tumble and trip over his boots and swords. But because his hair was black and shining, and his dinner-jacket correctly cut, and because he had done his best to deprive his speech of the country flavour which is necessary to clowning, the Spaniard had no longer blighted his life.

Everything seemed set fair for his future as an actor-manager, so fair in fact that he paid vast sums to be relieved of his future variety engagements. Then began an overwhelming run of bad luck, culmin-ating in his production of Edgar Wallace's "The Lad" in 1928. The autumn tour was so profitable that his fortunes were being restored, but the run at the Shaftesbury Theatre began at the time of the depres-sion caused by the illness of King George V. Even "The Spaniard That Blighted My Life" added to his burdens. As it happened to have been one of the songs which helped Al Jolson along the road to success it was included in one of his "singies" when he became a film star. Billy Merson claimed compensation, and was offered £2000. The case came into court. He won. Then there was an appeal, a technical flaw in the contract was discovered, he lost and had to pay the costs of both actions.

So Billy Merson resumed his famous "ginger" wig and returned to the halls in his old disguise. Later he came to the Palladium in a mass of blonde ringlets while serenading "Desdemonia," for whose sake he was risking pneumonia in classic simplicity of dress. The singer who created such a lasting testimonial of his popularity as "The Spaniard That Blighted My Life" should find that the British public is his friend.

VICTORIAN "GODS"

From a drawing by Maurice Greiffenhagen in "Footlights," "Judy's" Annual for 1895

SUNG WITH OVERWHELMING SUCCESS.

MR FRED BY COYNE.

"FULL INSIDE"

"WHO'LL OBLIGE A LADY?"

WRITTEN BY
V. PAGE.

Entered at Stationers' Hall.

COMPOSED BY
VINCENT DAVIES.

PUBLISHED BY J. BATH, 23 BERNERS STREET, OXFORD STREET, LONDON. *Price* **3/-**

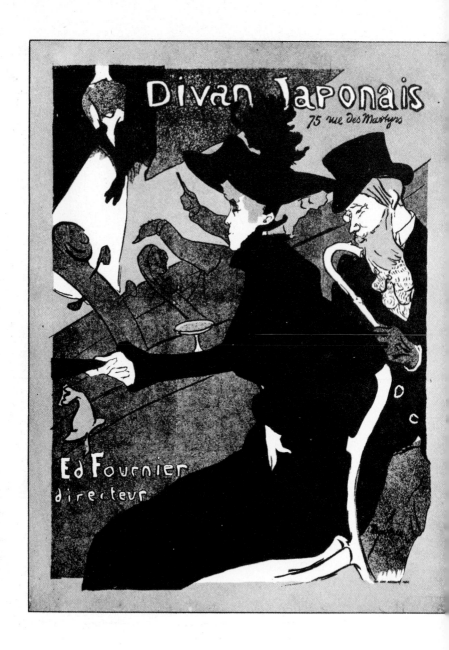

108 THE REVERED NECK OF YVETTE GUILBERT

(*On Reverse*) 107 CHIVALRY AND THE KNIFE-BOARD BUS

CHAPTER FIFTEEN

From Overseas

IN his battered topper, long black overcoat, high collar, white trousers with ragged ends, and boots that flapped on the stage as he walked rapidly up and down, R. G. Knowles was one of the outstanding figures of the old halls. Styling himself the "very peculiar American comedian," he liked to give the impression that he was a Yankee born and bred. Actually he was born (October 7, 1858) and educated at Hamilton, Ontario. Still, there was excuse enough in this for him to call himself "A Modern Columbus" in the title of his autobiography and to sing about "Columbus Up-To-Date." "Foreignness" was necessary to the comic idea of himself exploited in his performances. He had to think of himself as the stranger within our gates, clothed in his motley and given leave to speak his mind about people and places that he wanted to watch as the proverbial onlooker who sees most of the game.

At the age of twelve and some odd months, he was given two dollars a week to do odd jobs in a Mr. Henderson's general-store. "Richard," said the shopkeeper, "eat all you can, but carry nothing away in your pockets." Richard obeyed the first part of his instructions so thoroughly that Mr. Henderson thought to warn him by reading aloud from a newspaper the report of a boy who had died after eating a pound of raisins, whereupon Richard retired behind the counter, weighed a pound of raisins, added a pound of nuts, and ate the lot. The shopkeeper laughed, and the budding comedian decided to make him laugh still more. When Christmas stock was being laid in, he at once carried on a raiding campaign "so successfully as to preclude the remotest possibility of candy being offered for sale to the public." That general-store went into bankruptcy.

One day Richard's stepfather gave him a whacking with a stick. One other day Richard threw the same stick against his stepfather's ribs and left home for Chicago, where he became a window-dresser in a dry-goods store. Perhaps "Knowles's" might have meant to us what "Selfridge's" does, had not a doctor told him he had only six months to live. That verdict prompted travels to Colorado with a donkey, named Bolivar, who chose the canyon where they were to live by galloping about, rolling on the ground, eating the rich grass,

R   129

tail, ears and jaw all expressing the liveliest satisfaction, and walking with stately dignity to drink in a pool filled by a spring gushing out of the rocks. At intervals he would inspect the hut Knowles was building, "and direct comprehensive glances at the cooking utensils with which it was decorated."

Both settled down to a peace that was disturbed only by storms. Bolivar sensed the first. He stood with statue-like rigidity, all eyes, while his ears were extended at an acute listening angle :

After a moment's deliberation he turned abruptly, and pushing by me unceremoniously, entered the house. Reversing himself when inside, he took up a position in the rear and with his head on my shoulder followed the direction of my gaze.

At the height of the gale, a boulder from the nearest peak tore trees out by the roots, scraped its way across bare rock with a sound like a great shriek of terror, shot into space and fell into the canyon, whence some seconds later came the crash. Knowles turned his head, and Bolivar looked him straight between the eyes with a glance which said, "Well, can you beat that ?"

What decided this hermit's future was the sudden appearance of miners. Strange groups of men came struggling along, mounted and afoot, in wagons, and guiding pack mules, all converging upon one spot :

The vanguard of the cavalcade halted, and the rest, hurrying up from the rear, ran around like an army of ants in a frenzy of energy. Tents appeared like magic, and a real white city presented itself to my wondering gaze. . . . this settlement was no other than Silver City, commonly known, by those who created it, as Leadville.

There was a hotel, gambling saloon, and variety theatre all rolled into one. Knowles asked to be given a hearing as a comedian. "If you promise not to die in front of the people I'll give you a —— chance," said the proprietor. The salary was twenty-five dollars a week, doubled by money thrown upon the stage at each performance. Having recovered his health, R.G. decided to return to Chicago. At a farm-house where he stayed after the first stage of the journey, Bolivar became so popular that his master gave him as a present to the farmer's small boy. They all saw him off to the station, "the intelligent animal's ears working in wonder as the train, bearing me upon it, disappeared from view."

At twenty years of age, Knowles was back in Chicago, determined to be a professional story-teller. After several applications for work, he was engaged at a little hall where "twice daily" stood for "continuous variety" from 2 p.m. to midnight. The next rung on his ladder was the Olympic, Chicago. There he pleased his audience by telling them that if they did not laugh they were not getting their money's worth—but not the stage-manager, who strode on to the stage, growled, "If you haven't had enough of this, *we have*," and lugged Knowles away by the ear. The applause was increased by this finale, but Knowles was ordered out of the stage-door—and stayed away until he was told that there had been a mistake. The stage-manager had decided that the newcomer had been guilty of breaking the rules which forbade any artist to address the audience in a personal manner.

R. G. KNOWLES
From an "Entr'acte" caricature

The next year he was in New York at the National. The next ten years he was making steady progress in vaude-ville, in plays, and in Haverley's Minstrels. He joined Daly's company and tried his hand at Shakespeare, for when two players fell ill he was called upon to double the parts of the wrestler and the old shepherd in "As You Like It." He might have become a serious actor had he not quarrelled with Daly. That occurred in 1899. Two years later he came to London, opening at the Trocadero on June 13, 1891.

All the male performers in the bill had to share one dressing-room. Among them were George Beauchamp and Charles Chaplin, the father of Charlie Chaplin. Before it was Knowles's turn, his wife, Winifred E. Johnson, was making her London début as "past-mistress of the banjo" while singing a medley of coon songs and dancing at the same time. Next, Susannah Schaeffer balanced two lighted lamps on her feet and "made them do everything but go out."

Seeing his own number signalled to "an outburst of enthusiastic silence," Knowles walked on, and talked without a laugh for five or ten minutes. A waiter, with two glasses of champagne on a tray, began to pass in front of the stalls. Knowles fell into step and called out, "When you have one of those that is out of work send it up here and I will give it a job."

The champagne reached the stage-box, where a glass was held out. He took it, dropped it while handing it back, and told a bandsman who stood up to see the wreckage not to look, because "all that was useful I've stored in my inland revenue department." To the laughing audience Knowles said, "Now that we understand each other I will leave the stage. Mr. Eaton will play the introduction and I will come on just the same as if nothing had happened."

At the end of over half an hour he had to hang out the number of the next turn as the climax of his speech. During his engagement for sixty-eight weeks that followed, he deputised for Dan Leno at the South London for the "benefit" of Charles Godfrey, and succeeded only in quarrelling with the audience violently. Yet he played forty-seven consecutive weeks at the Empire, and two years and ten months consecutively at the Tivoli. Later he toured [1] South Africa, Australia, New Zealand, Egypt, Palestine, India, China, and Japan until his knowledge of the world became so vast that he tried to unburden himself as a lecturer before audiences who grew restive because he did not make them laugh. He remained our favourite "American music-hall comedian" until his death on New Year's Day, 1919.

*   *   *   *   *

As the "tabs" part, "Lustige Bruder" is being played. A door in the drawing-room on the stage opens, and Albert Whelan enters as elegantly assured, in evening dress, as he has always been these thirty years past or more (until he advertised, "No Hat—No Coat—No Gloves—No Whistle" in a new act). While setting down his silk hat, white gloves, and silk-lined overcoat, he whistles "Lustige Bruder" with a dexterity of note that the gallery boys have long tried to emulate without ever getting the knack of those warbled trills. Albert Whelan cocks an ear at their attempts, smiles sympathetically over their breathless failure, and looks at his wrist-watch.

---

[1] How the spirit of the music-hall had just been carried abroad is instanced by an adventure of Maurice de Frece while touring the Transvaal as "Professor Hoffman, Wizard of the City of the Golden Gate." In one small town, where no public amusements had been given for two years, the magistrate offered him the police court and the spectators brought their own chairs. According to Charles Douglas Stuart and A. J. Park in *The Variety Stage*, the magistrate was so well pleased that he said when the wizard came to clear the court of his fittings the next morning, "Never mind, I'll remand the prisoners," and did so for four days.

He has painted a problem picture like those by Collier that used to
propound a problem per year in the Royal Academy. Is he "all
dressed up and no place to go?" Is he merely killing time between
the cocktail party he has just been to and the supper engagement he
is just going to, or is he the victim of a heartless jilt, returning home
"me and my shadow" fashion, to wonder what he is to do? Years
ago we gave up trying to find that out, but the problem gave atmosphere to this deftly arranged act. The man-of-the-world, having
nothing better to do, tells us about the costermonger who decided
to sell some of his prize Victorian plums to the King because the
National Anthem commanded loyal subjects to "send him Victorias."
There are other stories, two or three songs, and a musical monologue
with comically inapt sound-effects "off"—notably for the ballad
about the courtship of the butterfly and the bee.

He was born in Melbourne in 1875, the son of Aaron Waxman and
his wife Eliza. After an education at the Church of England Grammar
School and Carlton College, Melbourne, he started life as an account-
ant and then turned mechanic. When gold fever broke out, he was,
while still in his teens, one of the first two-hundred-and-fifty to start
prospecting at Coolgardie, Western Australia.

"We lived on tinned food and condensed water for the first ten
months, and died like flies," he says. "It was in a tent out there that
I made my first professional appearance. I had very big billing—on
the trees. I painted my nose red and sang a comic song. That
finished, I jumped down from the stage and played the violin in the
orchestra."

On returning to Melbourne he was booked by McLellan for the
first Australian "Belle Of New York" company. The player of
Ichabod Bronson fell mortally ill, and young Whelan took his place,
giving so true an impersonation of the other that audiences did not
know the older actor was absent from the cast: when they read of his
death in the papers, they looked at his double on the stage and refused
to believe the report was true. From Australia, Albert Whelan
"jumped" to the Empire, Leicester Square, in the October of 1901.
That was when he invented the idea of signature tunes by whistling
"Lustige Bruder." Meanwhile, McLellan was rehearsing a London
revival of "The Bell Of New York." Remembering what happened
in Melbourne, he engaged Albert Whelan to play Ichabod Bronson
in London.

He was booked at the Coliseum when the management was trying
a policy of "four times daily." The first turn found itself whisked
out of sight on the revolving stage before it could begin. There were
protests, but the stage-manager had to keep to his timed schedule.
"All that I could do," says Albert Whelan, "was to rush on, whistle

my signature tune, look at my watch—and exit.   By doing that at
every performance, I earned the thanks of the management."

*   *   *   *   *

"Flanagan" was Florrie Forde's maiden name.   "Flanagan" was
one of her many chorus songs.   "Flanagan" was the stage-name of
the dame in her touring pantomime who has become one of the
leading comedians of the halls to-day.   For years she was the prince
of principal boys.   Now she is the queen of the chorus songs.   Who
wants to hear crooning while she is about?   There is nothing like the
grand pantomime manner for "putting a number over," and in this
she excels.   Even in mufti she still has the swagger of Dick Whittington
or Robin Hood.   If ever the Guards want to know how to march one
way while facing another, she should have the appointment (with
uniform) of H.M. Instructor to the Brigade.   Sergeants will envy
her knack of using one side of her mouth only and always keeping
the wide-open bit towards her listeners as she marches across their
front in a triangular series of strides.

She was born in Melbourne in 1876.   Very early in her 'teens she
went to Sydney to appear in one of George Reynolds's pantomimes.
Although she "had a name" he would give her only a part in the
chorus.   Twelve months later, while she was making a stir in Melbourne, he engaged her as principal boy, not remembering he had
ever seen her before.   "Somebody with no special charity for me
reminded him, with the warning that I had never spoken a line on
the stage," she says, "and he became decidedly nervous."   He wired
to Melbourne.   The reply was "True enough, but you've got the star
of the season."   And that is how she became a prince.

Through Harry Rickards, the London comedian who became an
Australian manager, she became known as "the Australian Marie
Lloyd" when a mere slip of seven stone.   As such she opened in
London on the August Bank Holiday of 1897 at the Pavilion, Oxford,
and South London.   She developed such an uncanny skill with
choruses that one night an audience made her sing a special favourite
thirty-three times.   All her choruses have the power to evoke bygone
scenes, old familiar faces, lost friendships and that elusive flavour, as
strong as sound or sight or smell, which our imaginations taste whenever dormant sensations of long ago come suddenly to mind.

*   *   *   *   *

Is Billy Williams remembered?   Although none of those who
once shouted his name from gallery, pit, circle, or "fauts.," will forget
him, he has no share in the legendary fame that makes some of our

idols loved even by those who never saw them. Yet he was among
the very few who could whip an audience to enthusiastic frenzy. I
remember a Bank Holiday performance when he was still being
called for after he had sung song after song. He had to leave, but the
shouting and the tumult would not die. No other turn could hope
for a hearing in that din. The management put on a prolonged display of living statuary. Pose after pose of chalk-white figures invited
our admiration. Instead we all went on shouting "Bil-lee Wilyums.
Bil-lee Wilyums," just to relieve our feelings, though we knew he
had gone. Soon he had gone beyond all earthly recall. He died in
the spring of 1915 at Shoreham.

Turn on one of his gramophone records and you will find that
infectious gaiety is still a living thing when his chuckle comes out of
the disc. He was one of the first to collect a gramophone following,
for he had that knack of putting his whole soul into the recording
which makes you feel the singer must be inside the box. "Why
Can't We Have The Sea In London?" and "Let's All Go Mad," pro-
ject into present and future that blithe irrepressible spirit of the past.
There was nothing much to look at in his turn—merely a curly-headed,
sturdily-built young man, rapidly swaggering up and down by the
side of the footlights, with flapping jacket to show the bright lining
of his dark blue-green velvet jacket. He was called "The Man In
The Velvet Suit." That was all he employed, unless you count
white spats, flowing tie, and a button-hole, by way of costume or
make-up.

According to Charles Wilmott's biographical sketch of him in the
Album of Billy Williams's Popular Songs, he was born in Melbourne in
1877. "The love of sport which was in later years to prove so expen-
sive to him found early development," it is stated here. He entered
a racing stable at Caulfield, and then became a boundary rider at a
squatter's station. His next experience of the turf was as a golf
instructor, "an epoch the brevity of which was owing not so much
to ignorance or want of facility in the language essential to the game
as to the fact that his brothers, Dick and Rowley Banks, were by way
of becoming professional champions of the Antipodes."

He joined a small variety company in 1895, and travelled the back
country, "playing in comedy, tragedy, vaudeville, and barns or anything else big enough to hold paying audiences which were principally
composed of miners and rough-riders, whose disapproval of anything
mean or villainous in the entertainment invariably made good for
the gunpowder trade." This led to a pantomime engagement, and
then to parts in musical comedy. In 1900 he started afresh in London
as assistant-manager of the Marylebone Music Hall. There he made
his first public appearance in England, and began to reveal his way

of inspiring song writers and composers to happy examples of "the wit of the wash-tub." At least one of his songs, "John, Go And Put Your Trousers On," was written and composed by himself, and in several others he took a hand. His spirit of cheerful nonsense is in them all.

R. G. KNOWLES

From a caricature by Max Beerbohm

CHAPTER SIXTEEN

Modern Music-Halls

In time you will feel irritable towards young people. They will deafen you with their zest for life. Out of a desire for self-preservation you will belittle all that they are up to. "Going to a music-hall?" you will ask in a quaveringly benevolent voice. And you will add, "Music-halls aren't what they were in my young days. Stars were stars then. There's nobody now to compare with Will Fyffe or Gracie Fields. Enjoy yourself—if you can." The room will be empty before your speech is finished.

I have no wish to be depressing. I mention this merely to show how we have always regarded the music-hall and always shall. We make it a matter for regret. We speak of it wistfully with a stifled sob in our voice. We want others to realise what they missed by not seeing the Great MacDermott and how much richer we who did hear him sing "By Jingo If We Do" are in spiritual experience. In short the music-hall is an excuse for bragging competitions in which everybody boasts how many dead performers he called by their Christian names.

That is why we pretend not to know that the music-hall still exists. We sigh for the veterans of variety who have gone, although we make no attempt to see those who survive. What we praise and what we enjoy are two very different things. We tell people that we hunger for the good old-fashioned halls and book seats for one where we can be sure to see some new thing. If all the old idols were still alive and still jesting as merrily as in their prime, many of the people who now lament their passing would not turn the corner to see them.

How the old order changed is best demonstrated by telling the history of the London Hippodrome, originally designed with a circus ring where Marceline would "help" the grooms to roll carpets before he went to the Hippodrome in New York, where he starved and at last shot himself. What the Dutch fisherman feels as he ploughs the Zuyder Zee may be mildly experienced by the middle-aged when they sit in the stalls which cover that arena now. Where you sit high and dry, frantic riders urged their mounts through a raging whirlpool at the time of "The Flood." In this less adventurous epoch we can feel the ghosts of our Eton suits looking down contemptuously from

S

137

the dress circle at adults reduced to seeing shows minus real horses—
in modern English "hippodrome" has no further use for horses—
and real water. It is nothing but a theatre now, and nobody on its
stage rivals our memories of the "experiments with liquid air"
conducted by the good Doctor Maxim Boyd, who cooked a steak and
boiled a kettle on a block of ice, or of the generous lady named
Norton who created gems out of common clay and gave them all
away.

Ransack your memories of a life of play-going and you will find
many a drama, farce, musical comedy, and revue reduced to dust
and ashes. Aquatic spectacles, on the contrary, have left visions in
your mind as vivid as the actual shows. Perhaps you will find it
difficult to say what they were about, but whoever cared a hang for
the plots? The moment we lived for in "Siberia" (1900 and a revival
in 1904) occurred when fugitives drove their sleigh by night through
the snowstorm down stage, across the bridge (over the place where
the orchestra had been earlier in the evening), and slap into the paper-
flecked waters of the tank, with Cossacks in pursuit.

Naturally, "Siberia" held the record, for even the throngs that
fled before the bursting of the tarn in "The Flood" created no effects
comparable to the agitated tinkling of the bells on that fearless sleigh.
"Treasure Ship To Fairy Seas" (1906) held no thrill at all, although
ingeniously devised with a circular transparency from tank to ceiling,
which was lit from within so that you had a good view of its sub-
marine scenery no matter where you sat. Annette Kellerman, chief
mermaid, never had a better setting for her lovely, casual dives.

For a long time the London Hippodrome grew up with our
generation. Directly we felt a little superior towards pantomime
round about 1904, it became superior too. Likewise, when we had
a passion in 1912 to be "new"—the word which expressed before the
War what "modern" stands for now—it reflected our spirit in
"Hullo, Ragtime." That was definitely, stridently, violently *new*.
None of the sensations of modernism has caused half such a stir.
Ragtime set friends and families by the ears. "Alexander's Ragtime
Band," "Everybody's Doing It," and "Hitchy-Koo" were played
on the whole plague of pianos that stunned the ears of peace-loving
souls before wireless was invented. It was all there was to satisfy
the wild demand for the *new* until Ethel Levy's voice swooped to
profound contralto depths and soared out again in the songs of the
revue written by Max Pemberton and Albert De Courville, and
staged by the latter as an example of what the new spirit could achieve
in the way of scenery and the handling of a chorus. No water had
been borrowed from the old "ditch" below the theatre for some
years. Over the trail of the heroic sleigh there was built the "joy-

plank"—new only in name, but new enough. If we dare confess our delight at seeing chorus girls dance past us, so near that they could have been touched, the derisive laughter of babes and sucklings would shame us. It was a thrill all the same when it happened for the first time.

History is told in the next titles. "Hullo, Tango" expresses the pre-War atmosphere (as recorded in "The Four Horsemen of the Apocalypse"). War broke out in the midst of its successful run. "Business As Usual," selected by the news-sense De Courville had developed as a reporter in Fleet Street, was the catch-word of November, 1914, when the civilian population was trying to make a virtue of its ignoble impotence. "Push and Go" was a quotation from Mr. Lloyd George's description of the kind of man the country wanted in 1915, and "Joyland," which succeeded it before the end of the year, sums up in a word the resolve to forget there "was a war on." "Flying Colours" suggests the extraordinary optimism which prevailed after two years of horrors, and "Zig-Zag" and "Box O' Tricks" the vacuity which followed disillusionment. Peace was celebrated with "Joy-Bells." Peace Night at the Hippodrome recalled the night of Mafeking. When the chorus lined the joy-plank and threw streamers at the people around them, a London audience for once gave outward and visible signs of enjoyment. Perhaps I did wrong to kiss the chorus girl, but as the impulse to apologise led to doing it again (and again) perhaps she did not really mind.

The War which has been held responsible for that negroid vogue of popular music, beginning with "ragtime" and culminating (at the moment of writing) in "swing," checked it if anything, for the British Expeditionary Force brought back to favour the music-hall song that could be marched to. It was the depression after the War that gave the second startling impetus to "jazz," and made Nora Bayes, a grey-haired matron with strict propriety in her appearance when at rest, the idol of the halls in London. She outdid all her forerunners in syncopation. She shouted, she strutted, she gibbered, she waved her arms like a semaphore signaller: she took us constantly by surprise because her behaviour could not be foreseen by following the trend of the song. She was expressive when she wanted to be. In "Dirty Hands" she made you see the imaginary child it was addressed to. But her characteristic style was derived from the antics of negro labourers on the plantations. His gibbering joy in moments of reaction against a life of misery did seem to resemble the amusements of a world where reality wouldn't bear thinking about, where comedians whose stock-in-trade still consisted of war jokes prompted in us no desire to laugh. Perhaps that was why Nora Bayes was the most significant figure on the music-hall round about 1924. All the stage triumphs of preceding years, whether won by actress or prima donna, were inconsiderable compared to the shouting and the tumult she called forth at every one of her performances at the Palladium.

Next came Sophie Tucker, less extravagant but more exuberant. The world seemed to be settling down, for though her background was New York the domesticity of it was universal. With her round happy face and a figure to correspond with the song, "Nobody Loves A Fat Girl, But Oh! How A Fat Girl Can Love," she seemed to be taking us back to "life down our street" or at least "our avenue." But she was definitely another example of *the voice*. There was no "dressing up," no backcloth, and very little acting apart from a very taking quiver of the lower lip. Meanwhile, American dance bands had taught their tricks to English bandmasters and an English girl had developed a style that beat the "torch-singers" at their own game.

Gracie Fields, whose maiden name was Stansfield, was born at Rochdale, Lancashire, in 1898. At the age of eight she sang in a cinema. That, she decided, was to be her life. In order to attract attention, she sang outside a boarding-house where "pro.'s" were known to be staying; and one did engage her to stand up in the gallery and sing the chorus of a song—a large woman in the row behind, knowing nothing of the contract, forced her to sit down. In one troupe of "juveniles" and another of "young stars," she added to her experience, but later there was nothing for her to do but become a girl in clogs and shawl at a mill. Yet at fifteen years of age she was a single turn, and celebrated her sixteenth birthday as the Princess of Morocco in "Dick Whittington" at Oldham. A touring revue brought her to London in war time at the dismal New Middlesex in Drury Lane, which was "The Old Mo" on its last legs. From 1918 to 1925 she toured (without missing any of the four thousand odd twice-nightly performances and matinees) in "Mr. Tower Of London," which brought her to the Alhambra half-way through that amazing run. As a mill girl who gave the magistrate in a police-court scene very sharp back answers she endeared herself to all. When she settled down as a star turn she retained her gift of humour, notably in her song about Uncle Ben, the self-made man who started life with a "coople o' dooks" and ended life with a "coople o' dooks." But there was no particular demand for this. Galleryites would shout for a dozen songs or more whenever she hesitated, but it was not among them. Her public, which lent a respectful ear when she was amusing them, worked themselves into a frenzy when she assumed the role of a sufferer from unrequited love.

There was an ever-growing passion for such ballads of inferiority.

For some years past the success of each season had been the melodious lament of a forsaken soul, usually all alone by the telephone, who asked, "What'll I do?" or "Why should you be mean to me?" or declared, "I'm all for you body and soul." Bill Sykes, leaning over the brass rail of the gallery, liked to look down into the eyes of Gracie Fields while she gazed upwards (into his, he thought) pleading for just one more chance of a little romance. Then you should have heard him shout! Once upon a time she used to burlesque sentimentality by uttering yelps and farm-yard noises at the most agonizing moment of an inferiority ballad's grovelling plea. She did this less and less frequently. The halls lost a first-rate humorist—handed her over to the films, in fact—while the gallery more and more noisily demanded its favourite "song hits" of the day.

This zest to hear the very latest song sung or played in the very latest way, has become feverish. Whereas the old "number" had a leisurely life of years, its modern counterpart exists only for some frenzied weeks. Yet during that brief period it dominates the music-hall where the dance band that plays it is the only serious rival to the crooner who sings it—into a microphone. There is never more enthusiasm than when a "best-seller" on the gramophone lists is starred. An act of this kind from the United States attracts, on its first night in London, ardent crowds eager to applaud the makers of their favourite records. Mechanised music, in effect, tops the bill.

The history of the music-hall is no longer the history of comic songs. Its leading comedians are rarely singers. There is one who composes songs for himself, but whenever he sings he lets that wistfulness which is rarely absent from fine clowning, dominate him altogether. Bud Flanagan jests only when he talks: directly the orchestra strikes up "Underneath The Arches" or some other lament of hopeless waifs, his earnestness changes the mirth of his bedraggled morning-suit grandeur into pathos. He was born at Spitalfields, and began his stage career as a boy conjurer at a trial matinée at Shoreditch. While performing as a blackfaced comedian under the name of Chick Harlem, he worked his passage to America and toured in "burlesque" until his return to enlist for military service. After the Armistice, he was engaged by Florrie Forde as comedian in her revues and dame in her pantomimes. When the tour ended he and Chesney Allen, another member of the company, decided to "make a book" at the dog races. Fortunately they were persuaded to start afresh in variety as a double turn.

In their cross-talk, he stumbles into verbal pitfalls at every breath. Whenever he has to be told that the right name for "Silverer's Black" is "Golder's Green," or that he is thinking of Ramsgate when he says "Sheep's Door," his partner, the orchestra and the audience shout "Oi" : and so he names his villa "The Cloisters"—not because it is "cloister the brewery" as in Gracie Field's song, but because he is so, he says, "fond of shell-fish." Here is a sample of his humour, printed as an explanatory note on the "souvenir programmes" of the pantomime, called "Gingerella," in the Palladium "Crazy Show" of 1931 :

You must all have heard the story of Sweeny Todd, how one day his father caught him with a Nax and said "What are you doing of?" "I want to be a sailor like you, Mother," answered the child, and they gave him a "Yo-Yo" and sent him to the Labour Exchange, where he became three times Lord Mayor (and HOW he could Lord Mayor!), however, he met a Madammois—a Madammois—a woman, and she said, "If you can find the one who owns this slipper I will make you a Millionaire." It would be a shame to give the plot away on a five years' lease so they built on the ground and it was the curse of India, years afterwards people will look up to his monument and say, "There was a brave man who mastered his 'Yo-Yo'."

Others among our leading music-hall comedians never sing—notably, Nervo and Knox. One, a member of the famous circus family named Holloway, stole his pseudonym from a pet monkey; the other, a son of G. T. Cromwell, the *improvisatore*, was nicknamed after a fall from a trolley. Burlesque ballets and slow-motion wrestling made them famous. Naughton and Gold were knockabout comedians before they had fuller scope in impromptu revels with Nervo and Knox at the Palladium where horseplay has been popular so long that here again we may suspect a public sensitiveness too delicate to permit jests at the grim realities of humble life.

The old music-hall vanished long ago. Its spirit was in the chairman, the *lion comique*, the *serio comic*, the tables, the waiters, audiences that threw things, and the exhausting mirth of winkles and champagne. Now the variety theatre which took its place is changing too. That has been effected by Mr. George Black, who came to the Palladium from the North, where he started life by turning the handle of a roundabout at fairs and gained his knowledge of showmanship from audiences that were the hardest to please in the whole country. In London he has fashioned entertainments of song-and-dance, conjurers, acrobats and jugglers, and all the other performers of variety, into shapes and patterns we have not seen before. His shows are popular, boisterous, alive : when they include veterans of variety it is for the sake of contrast, to prove that the vaudeville of to-day has a mirth of its own that marks it off from the music-hall of the past.

109 GRACIE FIELDS (AS SHE USED TO LOOK) AT THE PALLADIUM

Fox Photos

110 THE ROYAL VARIETY PERFORMANCE OF 1937 AT THE PALLADIUM

112 BUD FLANAGAN POISONS THE CUP OF JIMMY NERVO (*centre*) WITH THE CONNIVANCE OF JIMMY GOLD, IN " ONE OF THE BRAVEST",
Sasha photographs taken at the Palladium

111 ALBERT EDWARD CROMWELL KNOX AS THE GREAT LOVER AND JIMMY NERVO AS HIS VICTIM IN " ANOTHER EPISODE OF DON JUAN"

113 THE CHORUS IN ONE OF MR. COCHRAN'S MIDNIGHT SHOWS AT
THE TROCADERO

"Weekly Illustrated"

114 A CABARET AT GROSVENOR HOUSE

"Daily Mirror"

How rapidly we are changing still, was proved by the Palladium's thronged Royal Variety Performance in 1937. No other event in the history of public entertainments ever caused—broadcasting being the reason—so many people to stay at home.

"ROLLICKING RAMS" AS SUNG IN 1938

"The only boys to make a noise
From now till day is dawning.
Out all night till broad daylight
And never go home till morning."

*From a drawing by Sherriffs, by
courtesy of the "Radio Times"*

INDEX

(The numerals in italics denote the *figure number* of illustrations.)

144